AWESOME
ARCHAEOLOGY

D1102834

TOTALLY AWESOME ARCHAEOLOGY

NICK ARNOLD

ILLUSTRATED BY CLIVE GODDARD

■SCHOLASTIC

Scholastic Children's Books,
Euston House, 24 Eversholt Street,
London NW1 1DB, UK

A division of Scholastic Ltd
London ~ New York ~ Toronto ~ Sydney ~ Auckland
Mexico City ~ New Delhi ~ Hong Kong

First published in the UK under *The Knowledge* series by Scholastic Ltd, 2001
This edition published 2009

ISBN 978 1407 10832 2

Printed in the UK by CPI Bookmarque, Croydon, CR0 4TD

10 9 8 7 6 5

Contents

INTRODUCTION

Archaeology is dead awesome...

That's because archaeology is about dead people and how they lived in the past. It's about dead ruins – overgrown and abandoned to the bats and snakes, or buried in the earth. And it's about dead bodies mouldering in long-forgotten tombs.

And when archaeologists dig up ancient remains they come as close as anyone can to bringing dead people to life and talking to them about the past. Of course, archaeologists don't *really* chatter to skeletons or mumble to mummies – if they did you might think there was something odd about them. But it's an awesome fact that archaeology can (in a way) bring the past to life by showing you what ancient times were really like.

In this book you'll discover...

- what archaeologists *really* get up to (including their more embarrassing moments)

- what archaeology is all about and how it can get under your feet
- some awesomely huge discoveries
- how *you* can become an archaeologist
- bucketfuls and bucketfuls of dirty, disgusting earthy facts. Stuff like the putrid secrets of prehistoric poo and skeletons and sinister tombs and how to mummify your brother or sister.

And it all starts in the next chapter where you'll be meeting the lucky person who discovered the most famous tomb in the world and the archaeologist who made a dead body into a mummy. (He was really wrapped up in his work!) So dig into the next few pages – you never know what you'll turn up!

DODGY DIGGERS

Before you tiptoe into any tombs or get to grips with mummies you'll need the low-down on archaeology. Vital info like the story of archaeology and which archaeologist jumped over a cliff and what it's *really* like to be an archaeologist...

So where *did* archaeology come from? Yes, that's a good question!

EXCAVATING ARCHAEOLOGY

Archaeologists dig into the present ground level and as they go deeper they find older, buried objects. You see, earth and rubbish build up over time and so the deeper you dig the further back in time you go – it's a bit like eating a lasagne. (I hope your school dinner lasagnes don't ooze with ancient remains!) Anyway, we're going to dig through the layers of time and unearth the story of archaeology...

TODAY

Archaeologists work in teams. They use computers to sort out their finds and scientific techniques to discover how old their finds are ("finds" are the objects archaeologists dig up).

1969

An excavation in Illinois, USA is one of the first to use a computer to record data on finds.

9

1960s US marine archaeologist George Bass pioneers modern underwater archaeology. This proves that archaeologists can be really deep – and sometimes a bit wet.

1949– 1951 Grahame Clark is one of the first archaeologists to ask scientists to help explain what a place was like in ancient times. For example, plant experts advise on plant remains. (Well, what did you think they'd advise on – sticky buns?)

1950s Kathleen Kenyon (1906–1978) excavates Jericho in Jordan. She is one of the first to use radiocarbon dating (see page 51) to find out how old her finds are. They ought to use this technique on the jokes in this book!

1920s Leonard Woolley (1880–1960) excavates the 5,000-year-old city of Ur in Iraq. He's so careful not to miss anything that he uses a toothbrush and toothpick to remove the dirt. (Let's hope he didn't try to clean his teeth afterwards!)

1900 Arthur Evans (1851–1941) excavates the remains of Knossos, Crete and finds a vast palace with some of the world's first toilets (2800 BC). Of course, he's flushed with success.

Augustus Henry Lane-Fox Pitt-Rivers (1827–1900) is so rich that he owns more names than anyone else! Anyway, he's also a general and introduces military survey methods to make detailed plans of excavations showing the position of finds. Modern archaeologists use similar techniques.

1870–1890

Heinrich Schliemann (1822–1890) finds Troy and several lost Greek cities described by ancient Greek poet Homer. You could say that heroic Heinrich homes in on Homer's home.

1860

Italian archaeologist Giuseppe Fiorelli (1823–1896) digs up the ruins of Pompeii – a Roman city buried by a volcanic eruption. The bodies of people killed in the disaster have rotted, leaving empty spaces in the lava that covered them and then set hard. Fiorelli fills the holes with plaster to make casts of the bodies. Sounds dead fulfilling, doesn't it?

1840s

Austen Layard (1817–1894) finds the 2,500-year-old palace of the Assyrian kings in Ninevah, Iraq. He digs up gruesome carvings and sends them to London where people flock to see the tasteful images of people being skinned alive. (They're in the British Museum, if you fancy a peek.)

1798	French archaeologist Emile Botta makes similar discoveries at nearby Khorsabad.
	Fearless French experts study the pyramids whilst a battle rages. I'm surprised their mummies let them out!
UP UNTIL THE 1700s	No one digs up ancient remains except to find treasure or something pretty to collect. And this certainly wasn't anything like systematic modern archaeology.

Now start working your way back up the layers!

Awesome info

In the sixth century BC Nabonidus, King of Babylon, set up the world's first museum of ancient finds from his city. Archaeologists have been searching for this museum in order to put it in another museum.

Ask an archaeologist

If you ever chat with an archaeologist you could test their professional knowledge…

Answer:

Thomas Jefferson (1743–1826) was one of the first people to keep detailed archaeological records (before then people simply dug things up and forgot where they found them). In 1784, Jefferson discovered that a burial mound in Virginia had been built in layers. In the lower layers the bones were more decayed and seemed to have been buried longer. So Jefferson thought these layers were older. Well, you wouldn't call old Jefferson a lazy bones!

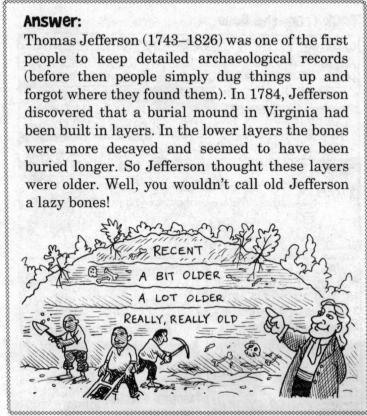

Early archaeologists made lots of mistakes. They didn't know how to work out how old their finds were, and often destroyed the remains they were excavating by careless digging. One archaeologist who was often mistaken was German Heinrich Schliemann. Let's imagine Schliemann was interviewed on the telly. Yeah OK, I know he died before telly was invented but perhaps the TV company dug up, I mean *excavated*, his body for the interview...

Back from the Dead

WELCOME TO THE PROGRAMME THAT DIGS THE DIRT ABOUT FAMOUS PEOPLE. TONIGHT WE'RE LUCKY TO HAVE WITH US HEINRICH SCHLIEMANN — THE DISCOVERER OF TROY

YOUR INTEREST IN TROY WAS SPARKED BY A CHRISTMAS PRESENT — THE WORKS OF HOMER . . .

COUGH, COUGH! I'VE BEEN DYING FOR A GOOD COUGH!

YES, HOMER'S WHERE THE HEART IS!

I WAS JUST TEN YEARS OLD WHEN MY DAD GAVE ME THE STORY OF HOW TROY WAS CAPTURED BY SOLDIERS HIDDEN IN A WOODEN HORSE. "DAD", I SAID, "I'M GOING TO FIND TROY." EXCUSE ME, I'M A BIT HOARSE JUST NOW... COUGH, COUGH!

WHEN YOU GREW UP YOU MADE A FORTUNE TRADING WITH RUSSIA

SO YOU DECIDED TO SPEND YOUR MONEY FINDING THE REAL TROY IN TURKEY

WELL, I WASN'T SHORT OF A FEW ROUBLES

YES, I WANTED TO SEARCH THE ROUBLE, I MEAN RUBBLE, AND I SUCCEEDED!

BUT YOU **DIDN'T** FIND TROY — IT WAS U.S. DIPLOMAT FRANK **CALVERT** WHO **TOLD YOU** WHERE TO DIG...

DETAILS, DETAILS!

AND YOU DUG TRENCHES THROUGH TROY AND DESTROYED MOST OF IT. YOU FOUND AT LEAST NINE CITIES, EACH BUILT ON THE RUINS OF THE ONE BEFORE, BUT YOU WERE SO EAGER TO BELIEVE THE SECOND CITY WAS HOMER'S TROY YOU SMASHED YOUR WAY THROUGH THE SIXTH CITY WHICH IS ACTUALLY THE MORE LIKELY CANDIDATE

ANYONE CAN MAKE MISTAKES!

RUINS

WHILST YOUR WORKERS TOOK A TEA-BREAK YOU SECRETLY DUG UP A HAUL OF ANCIENT JEWELLERY FROM AN ANCIENT GRAVE. THEN YOU DRESSED YOUR WIFE IN IT — AND ACTED AS IF THE TREASURE BELONGED TO YOU!

YES, SOPHIA MY LITTLE TREASURE!

YOU BROKE THE LAW BY SMUGGLING THE TREASURE OUT OF TURKEY!

I MADE A GRAVE MISTAKE

BUT YOU CAN'T PUT IT RIGHT NOW BECAUSE YOU'RE DEAD

WELL, THAT'S MY FUNERAL!

15

But not all archaeologists ended up famous and successful like Schliemann, so grab a hankie, read on, and have a good cry...

Unhappy archaeologists

1 Victorian archaeology expert JT Plight spent years making beautiful detailed drawings of prehistoric remains in Cornwall, England. But no one wanted to buy his work and as his money dwindled he went mad and had to be locked up. His Plight must have been desperate.

2 Native Peruvian archaeologist Julio Tello struggled to get into Harvard University, USA, to study archaeology. Driven by a powerful desire to discover his nation's history he returned to Peru and found a richly carved temple. Studying the temple became his life's work. One night heavy rain broke a dam and the flood swept away Tello's museum of hard-won finds and buried the temple in mud. Tello said...

THUS VANISHED THE DREAMS OF THE ARTIST AND ARCHITECT!

"And the archaeologist too," he might have murmured. Tello died two years later, a broken man.

3 Australian Vere Gordon Childe (1892–1957) put together the available information and figured that farming began in the Middle East after a dry spell caused a food shortage 10,000 years ago. Later, archaeologists found out that there was no such dry spell. As the evidence built up against him Childe got depressed and jumped over a cliff.

So what's it like being an archaeologist? Is it all doom and gloom or does the job have its brighter moments? You'll be finding out in a moment, but first – can you work out which of these is the GENUINE job advert for an archaeologist?

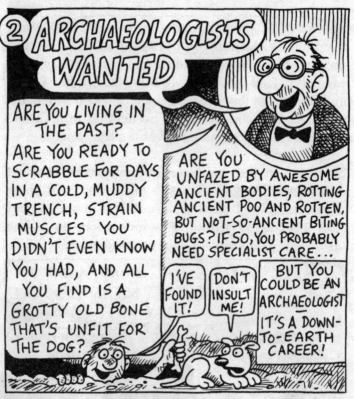

So did you spot the genuine advert?

'Fraid so. You see, being an archaeologist is hard work and it can be very boring and you don't even earn much money. But before you throw down this book and switch on the telly, read this…

wonderful things

Egypt 1923

The heat was stifling. Sweat matted the man's dark hair and trickled down the neck of his white, starched shirt and dripped on his grubby, white linen suit.

He was in his forties, a large thick-set man not given to showing his feelings, apart from short bursts of temper. But now his big hands were trembling. His name was Howard Carter and the whole of his life had been leading up to this moment...

The candle flickered in the musty air as he scraped impatiently at the small hole, opening a window in the crumbling plaster of the blocked-up doorway. What lay beyond? Was it an empty chamber or perhaps...

As Howard Carter worked, his mind filled with memories. He remembered washing dirt off finds as a teenager on his first archaeological dig. He thought of his years of working for the Egyptian government and searching

19

for the tomb of the boy-king, Tutankhamun. And he thought of the moment just a few weeks earlier when one of his workmen had found a flight of steps leading into the ground. Here, on the very last spot Carter had thought to look, was the lost tomb.

At last the hole was large enough to peer through. Oily smoke curled from the candle wick and the flame flickered in a sudden draught. After-images flashed before Carter's eyes and the dancing shadows seemed to glitter. What was it? Gold? Yes, it was the glitter of gold!

He heard a soft voice in his ear. "Can you see anything?" Lord Carnarvon, the man who had backed Carter with his own money, was anxious for news. He was a pale-eyed figure with a strained, pock-marked face.

"Yes!" Carter gasped. "I can see wonderful things!"

golden thrones carved like animals, gold painted statues, and golden caskets stuffed with jewellery. There was gold everywhere and treasure beyond his wildest dreams. Excited whispers filled the air as the news passed amongst the people waiting behind Carter.

But Carter was still staring into the room with a dazed look. He no longer noticed the sweat that trickled down his dusty face and soaked his shirt. He was gazing at a place that had been forgotten for 3,000 years – that's 50 lifetimes. He breathed stale air that had been trapped since the days of ancient Egypt. And Carter knew that his life had changed … yes, it had changed for ever.

In the coming weeks and months the discovery was front page news and the papers went wild...

Delhi News – November 1922
FIT FOR A KING!

Howard Carter has made the greatest archaeological discovery of all time! Archaeologist Carter, 48, said today: "This is as good as it gets!"

The Australian Sport – November 1922
TOOT AND COME IN!

Proud Pommie digger Howard Carter smiled by the Nile as he hailed the biggest bonza ripping treasure trove in history!

New York News – November 1922
KING TUT IS FOUND!

Howard Carter has made a real swell find. Unlike the other tombs in the Valley of the Kings, this one hasn't been turned over by hoodlums in ancient times.

THE CAIRO TIMES – MARCH 1923

LATEST NEWS FROM TUT'S TOMB

The tomb contains four rooms packed with thousands of priceless treasures including three golden coffins shaped like the king's body and placed one inside the other, a solid gold death mask, the king's personal furniture, clothes, jewellery and games. Said Howard Carter: "There's even more here than we imagined – it's going to take me ages to study."

And for more info on the finds in Tut's tomb see page 80

The story grabbed the public's imagination. It sparked new fashions for ancient Egyptian-style clothes, jewellery and decor. And, of course, the world of archaeology was thrilled too. Here's an archaeologist to explain why the tomb was so important...

As good as it gets

IT'S INCREDIBLY RARE TO FIND A LOST TOMB IN THE VALLEY OF THE KINGS THAT HASN'T BEEN ROBBED

ALMOST ALL EGYPTIAN TOMBS WERE ROBBED OF THEIR TREASURES IN ANCIENT TIMES

IT'S RARE TO FIND A PHARAOH'S MUMMY — MANY OF THEM WERE DESTROYED BY ROBBERS

LUCKY OLD CARTER (SIGH!)

KING TUT IS FOUND

Awesome info

And talking about mummies – mummy expert Bob Brier actually made his own mummy to investigate how the Egyptians did it. He cut open a dead body using replicas of ancient Egyptian tools and preserved the body using the same techniques and materials as the ancients. (You can find out what this involved on page 146.) Bob showed some archaeologists a slide show of the gory goings-on and some of them felt rather unwell. (Perhaps, like the mummy, they got a little wound up.)

MUMMIES THE INSIDE STORY

But there's much more to being an archaeologist than DIY mummies and finding lost tombs. Before archaeologists discover anything, before they can even start digging, they have to find a site – that's a place to dig. And that's what the next chapter's all about. So read on – it's a site for sore eyes...

SECRET SITES

You're not allowed to start this chapter until you've read the following important warning...

An important warning!

Archaeological sites can easily be damaged by careless visitors. Here are three things you shouldn't do (if you want to stay out of prison).

* * *

1 DON'T dig up the countryside. Chances are someone owns the land and there's a danger of getting your leg chewed by a savage guard dog – or its even more savage owner.

GRRR!   GRRR!

2 DON'T dig up parks or schoolgrounds. You might end up being chased by a murderous half-crazed park keeper – especially if your excavations destroy his prize dahlias.

3 DON'T use a metal detector to search for finds. Say "metal detector" to archaeologists and you'll get a dirty look and a few might even burst into tears. That's because some metal detector owners have actually robbed archaeological sites.

Still reading?

Great, now on with the chapter. I should point out that it's perfectly OK to look for archaeological sites just so long as you *don't* break these rules. And I know just the book to help you...

Archaeology for Beginners
by EC Peasy

Introduction

Archaeology, archaeology, archaeology. I LOVE saying that word. You see, archaeology is just so wonderfully, super-dupa-ly cool. I've been an archaeologist for 47 years and I still can't get enough!

The Author

It's great, wonderful, fantastic because you can do it without special gear or years of knowledge – and that's what this book is all about: archaeology for beginners!

Chapter 1: The Rite Site

So welcome budding archaeology dudes! The first thing you'll need to be an archaeologist is a site to explore and I know just how to find one...

Step one

Grab a map, unfold it (make sure the cat doesn't jump on it) and check a few place names. And get this – some place names give you clues to the local archaeology. I mean, imagine somewhere called "Bone Hill". It might just be a hill containing – hey, that's right! – bones. So maybe it's an old burial place? Street names may also tell you about an old site – guess what you might find in Castle Street or Abbey Road?

Step two

Hold it right there, dudes! Before you grab your shovel there's something else you just can't do without. Info – more clues as to what the site was used for! So make a bee-line for your local library

and dig up some facts. Has anyone found old pottery or coins on the site? Are there any creepy old legends? Old tales can provide clues about the history of a place.

Step three

Done that? Great – now it's check-out-the-site time! Take a little snoop around. Spot any worn-looking stones that might have been part of a wall? Stones from ancient sites were often re-used, so look for some in the walls of old houses. So how "wall" you get on?

Step four

It's time to test your detective skills to the max! Yes, it's eyes to the ground and take a good look (but don't go sneaking into gardens without permission). Here are a few things to look out for...

A line of scattered stones might mark the line of an old wall. Well, stone me!

Old pottery and bones on the ground. They're not any old rubbish – chances are they're archaeological old rubbish!

If you spot lots of this stuff it might mark the remains of a house or settlement. Well, that "remains" to be seen, ha, ha!

Step five
And whilst you've got your nose to the ground, why not get friendly with the local plants? I'm serious, plants tell you about the past if you look for crop marks. Whoops – a bit of jargon there – sorry, dudes! Crop marks suggest where a site might be buried…

- Tall plants may show the position of a ditch that has been filled in.

- Short plants may show a wall under the ground.

Step six

Just before sunset you may see something weird at the site (hope you're not scared of g-h-o-s-t-s!). (Younger archaeology dudes will need an adult with them.) Yes, the low light shows up bumps and hollows that you won't spot at any other time.

- A dip might mark a pit that has been filled in.

- A bump might mark the remains of a wall.

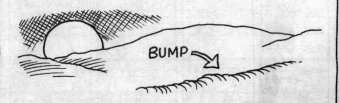

But dudes, mind you don't trip over any of these or you'll have an archaeological bump on your bonce!

Awesome info

1. Stinging nettles often grow on sites of old ditches or pits – they seem to like dug-up soil. Nettles also like soil rich in a chemical called phosphorus found in animal dung and bones – so a clump of nettles might hide an awesome archaeological secret!

2. English archaeologists are staging the world's slowest experiment. In 1962 they made an earth bank and ditch and buried various finds in it. The plan is to keep checking the site until 2088 and find how a real site changes over time and how quickly objects rot in the ground. The news so far is that the ditch has filled with soil and the buried fabric is falling apart.

SENSATIONAL SITES

Archaeologists find old sites using the techniques E C Peasy described, but many discoveries are made by chance. Farmers plough up fields and turn up old pottery, building workers dig the foundations of a new hotel and unearth skeletons. And people do stumble across sites – yes, I mean stumble. In 1982 archaeologist Francis Pryor found a 3,000-year-old wooden platform originally built over a swamp. Well, actually he tripped over one of the timbers sticking out from the ground. The remains at Flag Fen, Peterborough, are now open to visitors.

Once archaeologists have found a site, they want to know more. And there's a real fun way to do this – take to the skies! When you're on the ground it's hard to make sense of all the bumps and crop marks. But from a plane or helicopter you get a bird's eye view of everything.

You can see how the marks and bumps reveal the outline of an old building – yes, it's plane to see. And you might spot nearby sites and get an idea of how many people lived in the area in the past and whether they were living in farms or larger settlements.

Archaeological info

1 One of the first aerial photos of a site was taken of Stonehenge in 1906. In 1913, archaeologist Sir Henry Welcome rigged up a new hi-tech aerial device to photograph sites in Sudan. Oh all right, it was a camera tied to a kite – but it was cheap and cheerful.

2 In 1980, American archaeologist Kent Weeks made an aerial survey of ancient Thebes in Egypt. He and a colleague flew in an old bomber and took pictures by leaning out of the bomb hatch. Every time the plane rolled they nearly fell out – sounds plane crazy to me.

Checking out the Countryside

Archaeologists are keen to find out what the area around the site would have been like for people in ancient times. Which of these methods seem useful and which definitely isn't?

TRUE/FALSE

1 They examine the contents of an old rat's nest.

2 They look for long-dead beetles and snails.

3 They break open rocks to search for fossils.

4 They study ancient pollen (the "dust" made by flowers).

Answers:

1 TRUE. In south-western USA, pack rat nests contain dried pee and rat droppings and dead leaves which last hundreds of years in the dry desert climate. Archaeologists study the leaves to find what kind of plants were growing when the nest was made.

2 TRUE. Beetles and snails are fussier than the most pampered pussy-cat. The choosy creepy-crawlies only live in certain areas – some prefer swamps and some prefer woodland. By noting the ancient bugs they find, an archaeologist can get an idea of what the area was like.

3 FALSE. Fossils take thousands of years to form and any fossils an archaeologist finds would probably date from long before people lived in the area.

4 TRUE. Protected by a strong casing, pollen grains last for thousands of years. Since every type of plant produces differently shaped pollen you can tell what kind of plants grew in the area in the past. And since plants (like bugs) are choosy about where they live you get an idea of what the landscape and climate was like.

Is that clever – or what?

And now for some exciting news... An archaeological dig will be taking place *in these very pages*! In fact, it'll be happening as you read through this book, so you'll be the very first person to find out what happens! Look out for live updates from...

The Dead School

Part 1: A hole lot of trouble

Killem School was an ordinary, boring average school...

Of course, it had its share of mad kids and cruel teachers but then, what school doesn't? Amongst the children who attended Killem School were three friends, Oswald, Claire and Tom. And their teachers included the head teacher, Mr Snipe and their English teacher, Miss Meek.

But something awesome was about to happen. A terrifying secret was about to be unearthed. And it all began the day Oswald met with an embarrassing accident…

Detention essay
by Oswald
It weren't my fault! We was playing football and I was scoring a good goal when the ground opened up and I falled in. I might have been killed or something! But my teacher – Mr Boots – gets mad at me! So Mr Boots sends –

P.T.O

me to Mr Snipe and I get detention for recking making the hole and ruining the pitch! S'not fair!
PS. I fibbed about the goal – sorry!

Detention essay
by Tom

Oswald falls over and he goes down like a tonne of bricks. Well, I guess he might way weigh two tonnes of bricks. Anyway, he makes this big hole. Mr Boots goes wild and Oswald gets sent off! I say we can't play with a hole in the pitch and I get sent off too!
Yeah, that's the hole truth...
PS That's a joke – sorry!

To the Head Teacher

Dear Mr Snipe,
I am sorry to trouble you – but I have to inform you that Oswald did not make the hole on purpose. I looked into the hole and I think it might have been caused by a collapsing underground feature like a buried arch. Please could you let the boys off?
Yours very respectfully,

Claire Smart (pupil)

The school was buzzing with rumours that Mr Snipe wanted the hole filled with concrete. But someone (who may have had a name beginning with "C") had already tipped off the local archaeology service.

Anyway, the next day a group of archaeologists arrived to inspect the mysterious hole…

The archaeologists:

PROFESSOR HELGA DIGBY (TEAM LEADER)

SAMANTHA SMILIE

NORMAN CASTLE-FIELD ARCHAEOLOGIST

KEVIN HEAP

MAP

Professor Digby gazed into the hole for a while and then began to polish her glasses with a thoughtful frown.

"Hmm," she said. "I think we're dealing with the remains of the first Killem School. According to my research, it's around here somewhere."

"Cor that's AWESOME!" cried Kevin. "I can't wait to get stuck in! Let's get digging, Prof!"

The Professor gave him a reproachful look. "Kevin – you've been warned about rushing into things. We'll need a full geophysics survey and site report."

"Oh yeah, sorry Prof – I forgot," mumbled Kevin.

"I best start the measuring," said Norman, wiping his hands on his none-too-clean overalls. He searched in his pockets and pulled out some string, measuring tape and a pencil stub.

"Don't worry, it's sorted!" cried Samantha, flourishing her mobile phone. "The geophysics people are on their way and I've ordered a GPS for the survey!"

Norman stalked off muttering something about new-fangled inventions.

	Histoy project by Tom
	Researching a site
	Archaeologists find out the history of a
	site. I read this book in the library that
	said there was an old school on the site of
	our playing feild field. It was set up by
	this old woman called Margaret Killem. The
	children called her "one-eyed Meg" and
	she got sacked for cruelty.
	B Well done!

History project by Oswald
Making a survey

A survey is a map of a site
showing where everythink is.
That way you can mark where you
find stuff on your map. One
real wicked way to make a map is
using a GPS system — that
means Global ~~postoning~~
positioning system. A ~~commuter~~
computer tracks up to nine ~~sat~~
~~salt~~ satellites (things in space
what goes round the Earth)
using radio waves.

* Earth → satellite *ping!*

Then it works out where the
bumps and dips of the site are
to within 5mm — that's Mega-
cool! But some ~~ark~~ ~~archie~~
archaeologists draw plans using
measuring string and tape.

C Could do better

History project by Claire
Geophysics

Archaeologists use a wide range of geophysical techniques.

Magnetometry

According to the Archaeology Magazine I bought with my pocket money, a machine measures disruptions in the magnetic lines of force that surround the Earth. These effects might be caused by buried walls, ditches, pits and burnt areas such as an old fireplace.

Resistivity

In the Encyclopaedia of Archaeology (2000 edition) it says that an electrical current runs through the soil. If the current runs fairly easily there could be a filled-in pit or ditch where the soil is less rocky. If the current meets resistance it may be stones from a buried wall.

Ground penetrating radar

There's lots about this on the Internet so I'll do some extra work on this. This machine fires a type of radio waves into the ground. The radio waves bounce back from buried walls and a computer plots where they are. The trouble is you might find that the hidden wall is really a sewer pipe.

A Excellent work!

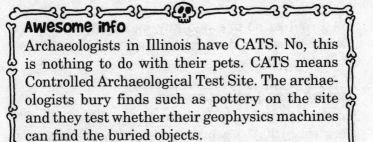
Now back to Killem School...

The geophysics people arrived and busied themselves with their machines and Samantha used a GPS program to produce a neat plan of the site on her state-of-the-art laptop computer. Everyone was impressed by the clear lines that showed up on the geophysics computer print-out.

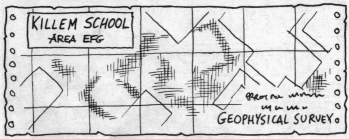

KILLEM SCHOOL
AREA EFG

GEOPHYSICAL SURVEY

"Cor!" said Kevin. "You can see walls and everything! And there's another wall that cuts across them all."

"That's a water pipe," said the Professor.

"I can't wait to get me 'ands dirty," said Norman gleefully. "This site looks like a cracker!"

"Well," said the Professor, "I think we can put in trial trenches here and here." She marked two neat lines on the print-out.

Of course, no one had any idea that there were dead bodies mouldering beneath the surface.

To be continued…

Making sense of your site

In the world of archaeology nothing is ever straightforward. OK, so you've surveyed your site and done your best to work out how big it is, and what shape it is under the soil. But you may not have the foggiest idea what the site was used for…

Awesome info

In Cornwall there are 3,000-year-old tunnels that lead to dead ends. Perhaps they were escape tunnels dug by school children, or might they have been underground toffee mines? Just like the tunnels, every theory leads to a dead end.

WE MAY NEVER KNOW THE ANSWER

Ultimately there's only one way to find out more and that's in the next chapter.

Ready for the dirty bits?

ENORMOUS EXCAVATIONS

Archaeology is as easy as burping. You dig a hole and grab the priceless old bits 'n' pieces and chuck 'em in a museum. Then you can put your feet up and read a comic for the rest of the day!

Archaeologists don't dig holes – they gradually uncover part of a site. And they don't "grab" anything – they gently lift the delicate finds. This is slow and painstaking work and not surprisingly many archaeologists limit their activities to small trial excavations to work out the site's layout. So how are the excavations going at Killem school?

Let's go and find out...

The Dead School
Part 2: A dig in the ribs
"Wicked!" said Kevin. "Can I have a go? Please Professor, I'll be ever so good – I won't drive it over no one's foot or nothing! *P-l-e-a-s-e!*"

Professor Digby shook her head firmly. "No, Kevin. You are *not* allowed to drive the mechanical excavator. For one thing you need a special licence..."

Just then the head teacher joined them.

"You're going to put everything back like you promised?" said Mr Snipe suspiciously. "Turf is expensive, you know."

The Professor looked slightly harassed.

"Of course we will – but we've got to remove the topsoil to get at the archaeological layers. This is the quickest and easiest method."

The driver started his machine and the noise drowned all further argument.

ARCHAEOLOGY TODAY
OCTOBER ISSUE
BACK TO SCHOOL!

A team led by Professor Helga Digby is excavating the remains of Killem School. Said the Professor, "It's unusual to find an early school that hasn't been knocked down and rebuilt. It's quite a learning experience for us all." The archaeologists are planning a full-scale dig and they have uncovered the remains of several walls.

"Professor!" yelled Norman from the trench, "I reckon I've found the slates that the kids wrote on."

"Hmm, fascinating," murmured the Professor.

"And look 'ere," said Norman excitedly. "This wooden artefact 'as preserved well – it looks like some kind of walking stick."

The Professor gingerly examined the fragile length of wood and rubbed a little earth from its shaft.

"I think it's a cane, Norman. It would have been used for beating the children."

Just then there was a muffled scream from the second trench.

Everyone ran to where Kevin was crouched. He was gibbering and pointing at an object in the soil...

"I, I, I..." he blabbered.

"You what?" said the Professor impatiently.

"EYE-EYEBALL!" he screamed, gesturing wildly at a small round object.

"Nonsense!" said the Professor firmly as she knelt down to examine it. The object was round and hard and creamy and made of glass. One side was painted to look like a human eye.

"Oh fancy that!" chuckled Norman. "An old glass eye. I've never seen one of them in the ground. But I'm more taken with that..." He pointed to a brown bump in the side of the trench. "I reckon that could be a skull."

"A SKULL!" Kevin shrieked and leapt out of the trench like a man who discovers a baby crocodile in his bath.

Just then a smartly dressed figure came jogging into view, her blonde pony-tail swinging...

"Well, guys," said Samantha, "have I got news for you!"

To be continued...

Awesome info

The position in the ground of every find has to be recorded, and every layer photographed and drawn. This tells archaeologists where objects were buried and allows them to work out what each part of the site was used for.

Awesome excavation quiz

1 When archaeologist J C Droop (yes, that really was his name) wrote an archaeology book in 1915 he said that men and women archaeologists shouldn't dig together ... why?

a) Because men are smelly in hot weather.

b) Because the men might swear and shock the ladies.

c) Because a woman's place is in the home.

2 What animal attacked archaeologists excavating in Ozette, Washington State, USA? Clue: this *wasn't* an underwater site.

a) A bear

b) A hamster

c) A jellyfish

GRRR!

Answers:

1 b) Tell that to your mum next time she says a rude word! With luck she'll say a few more!

2 c) Ha ha, trick question! The archaeologists used fire hoses and sea water to wash away mud covering the remains of an ancient Native American village. A jellyfish shot out of the hose and attacked the archaeologists on dry land!

Do it yourself ... your very own Dig

Here's your chance to try your hand at a little archaeology (just beware of vicious marine life).

All you need is...

- A patch of earth. It helps if you have permission to dig this up – and make sure it isn't in the middle of the pumpkin patch, the rose bed, or underneath your grandpa's deck chair.

- Gardening gloves.
- A trowel
- A large paintbrush
- Pencil and notebook

All you do is...

1 Put on the gardening gloves to protect your hands from germs. Make sure that any cuts are bandaged.

2 Gently dig into the ground, making sure that you don't dig too deeply in any one part of the hole. Use the brush to remove soil from around any objects that you find.

3 Draw a plan of the hole showing the position of any finds and the different layers of the soil. You can use these for dating...

Don't read on until you've read this bit: fill in your excavation afterwards. If your little brother/sister falls into your hole you'll find yourself in a hole lot of trouble and life would be the pits!

Did someone mention Dating?

No, we *won't* be digging the dirt on the murky private lives of archaeologists and what they get up to with their boy/girlfriends. You don't think you'd be reading about that kind of muck in a respectable book like this, do you?

No, archaeological dating means looking at objects found in different layers of a trench and working out how old the layers are. Take a close look at the layers of soil in the sides of this trench. (By the way you won't find all this stuff in a single trench. Well, not unless you're excavating a museum!)

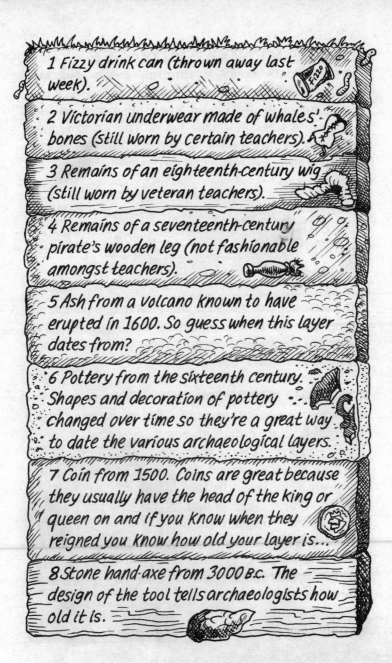

1 Fizzy drink can (thrown away last week).

2 Victorian underwear made of whales' bones (still worn by certain teachers).

3 Remains of an eighteenth-century wig (still worn by veteran teachers).

4 Remains of a seventeenth-century pirate's wooden leg (not fashionable amongst teachers).

5 Ash from a volcano known to have erupted in 1600. So guess when this layer dates from?

6 Pottery from the sixteenth century. Shapes and decoration of pottery changed over time so they're a great way to date the various archaeological layers.

7 Coin from 1500. Coins are great because they usually have the head of the king or queen on and if you know when they reigned you know how old your layer is...

8 Stone hand-axe from 3000 B.C. The design of the tool tells archaeologists how old it is.

A TREE-MENDOUS ADVANCE

Archaeologists enjoy examining grotty old tree stumps and bits of wood. But why? Well, every tree grows outwards putting on a new layer of wood each summer (it's called a tree ring). The same type of trees in a region grow by similar amounts and so they have the same pattern of tree rings year by year.

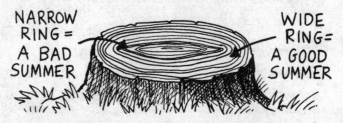

NARROW RING = A BAD SUMMER

WIDE RING = A GOOD SUMMER

Archaeologists can match the tree ring patterns on large timbers to computerized records and work out when the trees were growing – yes, archaeology really is branching out.

Remarkable radiocarbon

It's amazing what strange ideas you get when you're building an atom bomb. Scientist Willard Libby (1908–1980) was working on the project to build an atom bomb in the Second World War when he realized that different radioactive atoms decay at measurable rates. You see the bomb contained radioactive materials and... Er, hold on, this is getting awfully complicated...

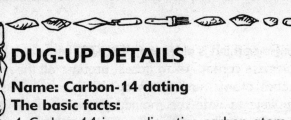

DUG-UP DETAILS

Name: Carbon-14 dating
The basic facts:

1 Carbon-14 is a radioactive carbon atom found in all plants and animals. Each atom gives out energy and slowly falls to bits.

2 Willard Libby calculated that it takes about 5,568 years (more or less) for half the atoms of carbon-14 in a sample to fall apart.

| DAY ONE | 5,568 YEARS LATER |

3 As more atoms fall apart, the sample gives off less energy. So by measuring this energy in a grotty old bone, scientists can work out how long the atoms have been falling to bits. And this tells them how old the bone is – clever, eh? Who knows, this technique might even work on your teachers!

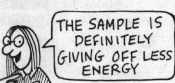

THE SAMPLE IS DEFINITELY GIVING OFF LESS ENERGY

The detailed bits:

1 After radiocarbon dating was discovered, archaeologists from all over the world sent Willard Libby bags of ancient wood so they could get a date on them.

2 When something is older than 125,000 years old you can't use carbon-14 to date it because all the radioactive atoms have fallen apart. This makes it impossible to date the mouldy prunes in your school dinner.

So far you might have got the impression that excavating a site is a bit of a doddle. You dig – OK, *very carefully* – and record what you find. But apart from the hassle involved in dating things it's all hunky-dory. No way! Archaeology can be awesomely awkward – just you read this!

Archaeological nightmares

These are all things that really have gone wrong!

1 Cute little rabbits can terrify an archaeologist. Bunnies burrow into a site and muddle up archaeological layers and confuse the excavators. Archaeologists thought that two layers of flint tool finds meant that prehistoric people lived on a site at two different times. Then someone pointed out that broken tools found in two layers fitted together. They'd been bamboozled by brainless bunnies.

I CAN'T UNDERSTAND THESE FINDS

OH, STOP RABBITING!

2 In many hot countries poisonous snakes live in ruins. At Troy, Schliemann found hundreds of deadly vipers. Huge poisonous spiders lurk in some tropical sites – I bet they cause a few hairy moments.

STOP IT, BERNARD! THAT TICKLES ...

3 Heavy rain spells bad news for archaeologists. If a trench gets flooded objects can be washed out of the soil. It's impossible to record which layer they came from and archaeologists might find themselves sieving sludgy mud for small finds and cleaning out the trench with a sponge and teaspoon.

THIS DIG IS A WASH-OUT

4 Sites in caves are dangerous. In some places the air supply is so bad it's actually hard to breathe – that's breathtakingly horrible! Oh, and the roof of the cave might cave-in – so I hope you're not craving for caving.

5 Stone Age people left very little behind for archaeologists to find except a few bones and stones (that's why it's called the Stone Age). Desperate archaeologists have been known to sieve every grotty handful of earth they dig in search of tiny finds.

6 In the 1940s, Iraqi archaeologist Fuad Safar and Briton Seton Lloyd excavated the remains of 11 temples, each one built on the ruins of the others. And if that sounds confusing, get this – the temples were built from mud bricks (sun-baked mud used for building in parts of the Middle East). And the bricks looked (how did you guess?) rather like mud, so the archaeologists had to grovel in the dirt and separate the mudbricks from the mud with their *fingertips*.

7 Theft can be a problem. Forty thousand tablets were snatched from one site in Iraq in 1877–1878. (These were blocks of clay used for writing and not headache tablets. Mind you, the theft must have caused a few headaches.) When archaeologist Thurston Shaw found beautiful bronze statues in a Nigerian tomb in 1959 he decided to put them under his bed for safe-keeping – but that didn't stop someone trying to steal the statues.

8 Deep trenches can collapse and bury archaeologists alive. For safety, trenches must be shored up with metal or dug with steps so that the excavators can escape.

ANYONE SEEN BASIL?

9 But *any* trench can be treacherous. When Leonard Woolley was excavating in Syria in 1912, a workman sneaked into a trench for a crafty cigarette. Just then a boulder balanced on the edge of the trench fell on his head and killed him. Proving that smoking really is bad for you...

Awesome info

Archaeologists in York excavated a Roman sewer and you know what it contained! Near the toilets they found dead Roman sewer flies and also grain beetles suggesting that the sewer drained waste from a grain store. Would you volunteer for this dig – or would that be going against the grain?

I'D KICK UP A BIT OF A STINK!

The lost legend quiz

One exciting thing about excavation is that archaeologists can sometimes check legends from the past.

Which of these stories is true and which is false?

1 My name is mud

According to Roman writer Aelius Aristides:

ME AND TWO FRIENDS WENT TO THE TEMPLE AT PERGAMON. IT WAS WINTER AND WE WERE FEELING ILL BUT THE PRIESTS SAID THE GOD OF HEALING WANTED US TO WALLOW IN MUD AND RUN ROUND THE TEMPLE THREE TIMES AND JUMP IN A FREEZING COLD SPRING! OH THE JOYS OF SPRING – I DON'T THINK!

YER WHAT?

COULDN'T WE HAVE A NICE HOT BATH?

I'D SETTLE FOR A WEEK IN BED

2 The well of death

The ancient well at Chichen Itza, Mexico, was used for human sacrifice. The priests of the local Toltec rulers threw beautiful girls down the well and they drowned.

MY SISTER'S BETTER LOOKING THAN ME!

Answers:

1 TRUE. Aelius tried the cure and felt better – but one of his friends had to be taken to the bathhouse to defrost. Would you fancy this treatment?

Archaeologists excavated the temple and found the spring and the bathhouse just as Aelius described them.

2 FALSE. Fearless US archaeologist Edward Thompson (1856–1935) dived in the well's murky waters in 1909. He burst an eardrum but only found a few mouldy bones.

Thompson had the water drained and found that people *of all ages* had been thrown in the water but mostly *after* the Toltecs had left the site. The Toltecs mainly chucked in jewellery for their gods. Well, well, what a surprise…

But there are some underwater places that are so horrible you'll be *begging* to be sent back to the well of death! I'm talking about the bottom of the sea in freezing murky water where the currents can sweep you away and sharks eat you for breakfast!

Fancy a dive into the next chapter?

MURKY MARINE ARCHAEOLOGY

In 1879, a heroic vicar named Odo Blundell wriggled into a rubber suit, plonked a heavy metal helmet on his head and descended into a very murky Scottish Loch breathing through a rubber tube. He must have looked really *Odo*!

HOOTS MON, IT'S THE MONSTER!

The vicar was a pioneer of marine archaeology – this means (don't faint with amazement) doing archaeology underwater! Oh, so you knew that?

Ah, but do you know the *full* watery details?

DUG-UP DETAILS

Name: Underwater archaeology
The basic facts:
1 It's hard to excavate if you're tied to the surface by a rubber tube and that's why underwater archaeology only made a splash after the invention of the aqualung in 1943.
2 Aqualungs use air cylinders linked to a face mask and a mouthpiece that allows you to breathe air underwater.

The detailed bits:

Odo Blundell studied the sunken remains of 1,500-year-old island settlements known as crannogs. One day a storm blew up and Odo thought a lake monster was after him – well, I guess Lochjaws can be fatal! He became so scared he gave up diving. It was a Nessie-sary step...

> GOOD! HE CAN GO AND ANNOY SOMEONE ELSE!

Essential equipment

And here's the gear you need to be a well-equipped marine archaeologist.

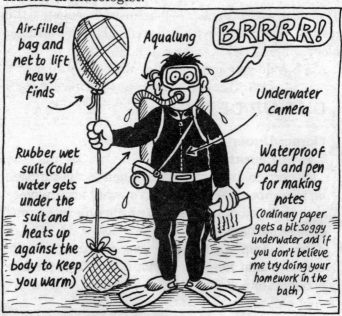

Air-filled bag and net to lift heavy finds

Aqualung

BRRRR!

Underwater camera

Rubber wet suit (Cold water gets under the suit and heats up against the body to keep you warm)

Waterproof pad and pen for making notes (Ordinary paper gets a bit soggy underwater and if you don't believe me try doing your homework in the bath)

Answers:

1 Yes, I mean *no*. That *is* an airlift but the archaeologist is talking about a machine that uses air pressure to suck water up a pipe to the surface together with sand from around a wreck. Special sieves catch any finds that get sucked up.

2 No, a prop wash is a tube linked to a boat's propeller that forces clear water from the surface to the bottom. There it can be used to wash away sand and mud from a wreck.

UnDerwater quiz

Underwater archaeology is an awesomely involved business. Here's a plan of the stages needed to excavate this fascinating wrecked galleon…

All *you* have to do is put them in the right order:

a) Start raising the finds and treasure!

b) Study the tides and currents of the area to work out the safest way to work.

c) Lay a grid over the site of the wreck.

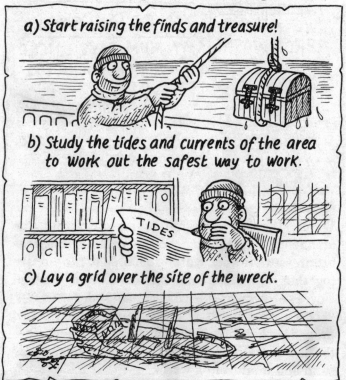

d) Use underwater radar and magnetometer machines to map the position of the wreck.

e) Look at old documents to find out more about the wreck and where it sank.

Answer:

The correct order is e), b), d), c), a).

1 e) You need to know where to look before you start looking. The records may tell you where the vessel sank and what cargo was aboard.

2 b) Safety is vital and you need to know whether the tides and currents have shifted the wreck on the seabed.

3 d) These can help you find the wreck. It may be completely buried in sand or mud.

4 c) It's vital to map your finds to try to make sense of a wreck that is often little more than a few scattered timbers.

5 a) At long last! And that's when your problems really begin (see over the page if you don't believe me).

DEEP TROUBLE

Underwater archaeology may sound glamorous and fun but it's actually a hard, dangerous business. Here are just a few things that can go wrong...

1 Marine archaeology isn't cheap. All your diving equipment has to be bought or hired and a ship has to be hired to dive from. And when you get to the site, the weather might be stormy or there might be dangerous underwater currents. If so no one can even venture into the water and try out all that expensive gear.

2 Sometimes the water is so muddy and murky that the divers can't see anything. Archaeologists working on a wrecked ship off Ningbo, Korea, could see nothing and relied on touch to find thousands of objects including 28 tonnes of Chinese coins. Oh well, at least they had enough change for the bus.

3 The deeper you dive, the more a chemical in air called nitrogen builds up in your blood. If you surface too fast the nitrogen forms bubbles that can block blood vessels and kill you. (This condition is called the bends.) The only way to get up safely from deep down is to rise in fairly slow stages, breathing a special mixture of gases to allow your body to get rid of the nitrogen. And you thought diving would be a gas...

And talking about danger, just read this story. It will have you spluttering into your snorkel.

The Cave of Death

Marseilles, 1991

Henri Cosquer had a secret. A secret so incredible, so amazing and so dangerous that people could die if they ever discovered it. And perhaps the worst had already happened. It was time to come clean...

"No news? OK, ring me if they turn up." The coastguard swore as he slammed down the phone. He took a deep breath and eyed Henri warily.

"I understand that you discovered the cave, Monsieur Cosquer. You informed the authorities and the missing divers went to see for themselves. Well, you had better tell us where to find them. We are still looking although..."

Henri held up his hand. "Monsieru, I am sorry to say that the divers are almost certainly dead."

The coastguard sighed bitterly and shook his head. "I knew it – their air would have run out by now. You had better tell me everything you know."

Henri took a deep breath. Should he have kept quiet about the cave? he wondered. Maybe it would have been for the best. If he had said nothing the three divers would still be alive. But it was too late for regrets...

"About six years ago I was diving off Cape Morgisu and I found the entrance to an underwater cave."

"And you didn't tell anyone?"

"No, the cave is a maze of tunnels – someone could get lost in them and drown for lack of air and..." Henri pictured the small underwater entrance and the narrow flooded  tunnels leading into the dark, into the unknown. "and ... I thought it was too dangerous to tell others. If people went there they might be killed."

The coastguard reached for the phone.

"So it appears, Monsieur Cosquer. You are willing to show us this cave – yes?"

And without waiting for a reply, the official picked up the receiver and started dialling.

"This is the place!" shouted Henri above the roar from the engine of the coastguard's boat.

The engine spluttered out in a whiff of petrol and they could hear the waves splashing against the limestone cliffs. The water looked deep and murky blue as Henri and two other men made their last checks before diving. Then they rolled over the side with loud splashes and began to swim underwater, Henri in the lead.

Henri never got used to the strangeness of diving – how the waves and sounds of the surface became muffled and lost in the explosions of bubbles from his mouthpiece. The way that the light turned from white to twilight blue. And suddenly there it was – he pointed out the rocky cleft.

Then Henri thought of what they might find inside and his heart began to pound...

He had been this way many times before. Always alone. If only it could have stayed that way! The three men snapped on torches and squirmed through the opening. Inside it was dark and the light of their torches was lost in billowing clouds of mud stirred up with every movement. The tunnel twisted and it was easy to lose your way. Henri thought of the missing divers and shivered. Then, a moment later, he saw them.

His light shone on a figure and then two more, swaying like drunks in the dark water. The divers were dead – they had lost their way and run out of air. Henri tried not to think of their final moments of panic and gasping fear. The three men had dived in search of the cave's secret – a secret so wonderful they had risked their lives to gaze upon it. They had died before they got there. Now it only seemed right for Henri to show his companions what that secret was.

Henri signalled the others to follow and brushed past the dead men. He tried to avoid their blank eyes and pale, clutching fingers. At the end of the passage was a crack in the rock. It looked like a dead end but it led into another passage – one so narrow that you had to wriggle through it like an eel. After what seemed ages it opened into a ghostly underwater landscape. Henri saw stalactites suspended in the gloom like daggers.

It was a drowned cave.

Close to the ceiling there was a ripple of light and Henri swam towards it. He surfaced and pulled off his face mask, and took a deep breath of cool air trapped by the sea over 10,000 years ago. Then he shone his torch around the walls. The other men joined him, and their mouths opened in wonder. There were gasps of surprise, and one of them said, "I don't believe it!"

The walls were alive with beasts. There was a huge ox drawn in ochre and red and arching its back. Deer trotted through the shadows. Horses reared and plunged and a seal twisted with its flank pierced by a spear. And strangest of all, they saw a human hand raised in greeting and outlined in blood red. It might have been painted yesterday.

This was Henri's hidden kingdom – a sunken art gallery 27,000 years old. Day after day the diver had returned to feast his eyes on the beautiful picture animals. But now he had shown others and the spell was broken. And Henri felt sad because this magic place was no longer his secret.

But were the paintings *genuine?* What do you think...?

a) Don't be daft! Stone Age people couldn't have reached the cave without diving equipment. Henri Cosquer was a brilliant artist who painted the animals for his own amusement.

b) Stone Age people invented underwater diving. Archaeologists think they breathed air stored in smelly pigs' bladders.

c) The cave had actually been on dry land but the sea level had risen and covered it. The paintings had been perfectly preserved in the underwater bubble.

Answer:
c) Today archaeologists can study the paintings – that's if they're brave enough to venture into the deadly maze of passages.

Fragile finds

1 Underwater archaeologists have salvaged some amazing objects. In the 1970s divers excavating the *Mary Rose*, an English ship that sank 350 years ago, found loads of wooden objects including a mallet used to knock people out before surgeons sawed off their legs. If this rare item were for sale it would cost an arm and a leg.

2 A diver found the remains of pork for a sailor's lunch. The meat had rotted into sickening slime and afterwards the diver smelt so bad that no one wanted to sit near him.

3 Wooden finds are always a pain. If the wood dries, it shrinks and splits and crumbles to dust. The only

70

way to protect it is to soak it in water and chemicals for months or years. For years after it was raised from the seabed, the wreck of the *Mary Rose* had to be doused in water to protect the timbers.

AT THIS RATE, WE MAY AS WELL HAVE LEFT HER IN THE SEA!

4 The Swedish ship *Wasa* was raised in 1961 after more than 300 years with her hull complete except for 14,000 loose bits. Wooden you just give up on it?

Awesome info
The *Mary Rose* can now be visited in Portsmouth, England, and the *Wasa* is on public display in Stockholm, Sweden.

Some good news about underwater archaeology

OK, so underwater archaeology is hard and dangerous. But at least you don't come across too many gruesome sights. Dead bodies are eaten by sea creatures and the bones rot. But on dry land there are tombs packed with the rotting remains of the ancient dead.

Nothing, I repeat *nothing* will prepare you for the next few grisly pages...

Welcome to the *Bone Zone*!

TERRIBLE TOMBS

There's something rather strange about building a whopping great tomb for a dead body. I mean who's going to *live* there? Are they going to thank you for it? Why not dig a pit and tip the body into it? It's a hole lot simpler!

MAYBE WE SHOULD MAKE THE PIT A BIT DEEPER

Well, archaeologists searching for finds are grateful that we humans feel that dead people require a bit more dignity. Most people in the past believed in some kind of afterlife and felt that the dead person needed to take a few bits and pieces with them. Things like food, clothes, weapons, a few specially killed servants and maybe the family pet...

Awesome info

Oh yes, it's true. Killing the family pet and putting its body in the tomb was very common. For example, a puppy was found in a 12,000-year-old grave in Israel. Well I'll be dog-gone!

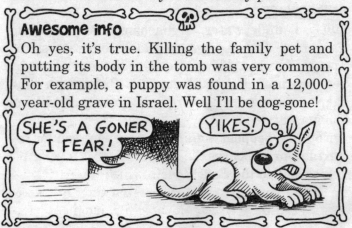

SHE'S A GONER I FEAR!

YIKES!

Three things you Don't have to reaD unless you like Being BurieD in Detail

1 The posh name for a coffin case (usually made of stone) is a sarcophagus (sar-coff-fag-gus). The word actually means "flesh-eating stone" in Greek because the ancient Greeks believed that the rotting body was being scoffed by the stone. Well, stone me!

I WOULDN'T SIT ON THAT IF I WERE YOU...

2 The biggest collection of ancient tombs in the world is the Theban Necropolis in Egypt. It's vast – over nine square kilometres (four square miles) of mouldering ancient bods. By the way, necropolis means "city of the dead" in Greek – just in case you were wondering.

WELCOME TO NECROPOLIS PLEASE DIE CAREFULLY

3 Some people were actually buried alive! Archaeologist George Reisner (1867–1942) excavated tombs in the Sudan, Africa, in which the position of the skeletons appeared to show that they suffocated after being buried alive. Meanwhile, judging by food remains found outside, the mourners were sitting down to a delicious dinner.

Morgue food anyone?

TOP TOMBS

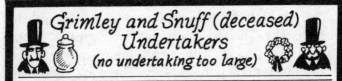

Grimley and Snuff (deceased)
Undertakers
(no undertaking too large)

Dear Customer,
Thank you for requesting details of Grimley and Snuff's De luxe Tomb Guide. You are obviously a person of discerning judgement, good taste and lots of dosh. Here you'll find everything you need for a happy afterlife. You'll be dying to try our latest designs based on archaeological discoveries.
Your most humble servant,

Ebenezer Grimley

PS Our customers never complain.

De luxe Tomb Guide
The best tombs in the world
(and probably the next world too).

Magnificent Mounds

(as built by Native Americans of the south-east and mid-west USA up until the eighteenth century)

Build your house on a mound (lovely view). When you die your house is burnt down and you're buried in the mound.

Everyone enjoys a feast (except you).

Your family strangles a few servants to keep you company in the afterlife. It can be dead boring stuck in a mound on your own.

Superior Ships

Fond of your private yacht? Why not be buried in it? As inspired by the Gokstad ship burial in Norway. Don't forget to be buried with all your weapons and valuables including your 12 horses, six dogs and a peacock.

The Ur Special

(As practised in Ur, Iraq, 2700 BC)
There's loads of room outside this rock-cut tomb for your servants, carts, oxen, etc.
You could have your very best friends walled up alive in the tomb – they'll be dying to be with you! (It's only fair to give them some poison as it's no fun waiting for the air to run out.) Form all the servants, oxen, etc. into a queue and make the servants drink poison (tell them they'll be falling in with a nice crowd). Bury the whole lot. OOPS nearly forgot – get someone to kill the oxen. You don't want them "lowing" the tone of the event!

SO, HAVE YOU DECIDED TO COME TO MY FUNERAL?

UR...

The Ch'in De Luxe

Grimley and Snuff regret that this tomb is only available by special order. We're only going to build it if you are either...
1 a billionaire
2 the Emperor of China.
And we want the cash up front. (You can't take it with you!)
Enjoy the ultimate afterlife experience!
Huge burial mound that took 700,000 people over 20 years to build.
5 km (3 miles) wall round the site.

A really roomy tomb with giant map of China inside with rivers and seas made of liquid metal mercury.

Life-size army of over 7,000 warriors individually modelled in pottery by 85 top artists. Plus over 100 war chariots and 600 pottery horses.

High-tech security devices: hidden crossbows fire arrows at any tomb robbers.

NOTE:

We're only going on old reports because the tomb has never been excavated. Chinese archaeologists say it's too important to rush into – but rumour has it that they're scared of meeting the old Emperor's ghost!

Accessories section

Nothing to wear in the afterlife? Don't despair – choose from our range of funeral gear as worn by well-dressed bodies everywhere!

The Pacal

Jade mosaic mask with artificial eyeballs as worn by Maya ruler Pacal the Great 1,300 years ago.

Note: Jade is supposed to keep your body moist and help you come back to life in the afterlife. It won't – but, hey, don't feel jaded, you've got style!

The jade suit

Liked the jade mask? You'll love this 2,000-year-old Chinese jade suit made from thousands of individually shaped jade pieces sewn with gold wire.

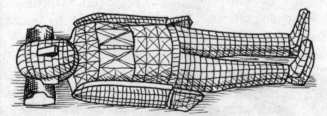

Gents' version as made for Liu Sheng, the Emperor's brother.
Ladies' version as made for Tou Wan, his wife.

I FEEL A BIT POORLY TODAY

OK. I'LL ORDER THE SUIT THEN

The lead coffin

Popular in the Middle Ages. The coffin is guaranteed air-tight and gases given out by your rotting remains can't escape. If anyone tries to open your coffin the gases mix with air and explode, splattering the intruder with foul green slimy bits.

GLOOP!

Of course if you happen to be a dead emperor or pharaoh you'll want more than a whopping great tomb, a few dead retainers, a lead coffin or a jade suit. You'll want to take into the afterlife all the goodies and luxuries you enjoyed in this life. Here's an ancient Egyptian document we unearthed. OK, it's probably a forgery...

KING TUT'S WILL

I, TUTANKHAMUN HEREBY ORDER THAT WHEN I DIE I SHOULD BE BURIED WITH THE FOLLOWING ITEMS...

SOME JARS OF MY FAVOURITE VINTAGE WINE (HIC!).

ALL MY CLOTHES AND FURNITURE (DON'T FORGET MY THRONE).

HUNDREDS OF MODEL SERVANTS (THEY'LL COME ALIVE AND SERVE ME IN THE NEXT LIFE).

A STATUE OF ME (IT'S NICE TO HAVE SOMETHING BEAUTIFUL TO LOOK AT).

MY PERSONAL WALKING STICK JUST IN CASE I FANCY A STROLL AROUND MY TOMB.

MY FAN IN CASE I GET HOT.

ONE SHOULD ALWAYS HAVE SOMETHING SENSATIONAL TO READ WHEN ONE IS DEAD – SOME BOOKS OF MAGIC SPELLS TO BRING ME BACK TO LIFE MIGHT BE HANDY.

ALL MY JEWELLERY.

LOTS OF YUMMY FOOD TO EAT (YOU CAN WORK UP QUITE AN APPETITE BEING DEAD).

A BOX OF ROSES (I MIGHT LIKE TO TAKE UP FLOWER ARRANGING).

A LOCK OF MY GRAN'S HAIR – MAKE SURE YOU FIND IT EVEN IF YOU HAVE TO COMB THE PALACE.

When people talk about ancient Egyptian tombs it's easy to imagine beautiful wall paintings, heaps of treasure and mysterious mummies. *Piffle!*

Actually, archaeologists were lucky that most of the objects in Tut's tomb were well preserved. Egyptian tombs can be awesomely unpleasant, as you're about to find out...

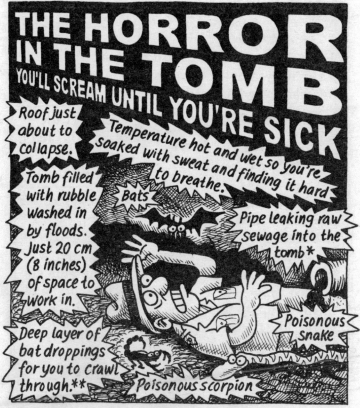

THE HORROR IN THE TOMB
YOU'LL SCREAM UNTIL YOU'RE SICK

Roof just about to collapse.

Temperature hot and wet so you're soaked with sweat and finding it hard to breathe.

Tomb filled with rubble washed in by floods. Just 20 cm (8 inches) of space to work in.

Bats

Pipe leaking raw sewage into the tomb*

Poisonous snake

Deep layer of bat droppings for you to crawl through.**

Poisonous scorpion

*At tomb KV5 in Egypt a modern pipe to a septic tank had been cut through the tomb and had leaked its disgusting contents. And yes, the archaeologists did have to crawl through this to get into the tomb. Was this the grave of Poo-tank-amun?

**Egyptian doctor Abdel Latif reported that in 1200 the Great Pyramid of Giza was full of bat dung. The stink was so awful that Latif fainted.

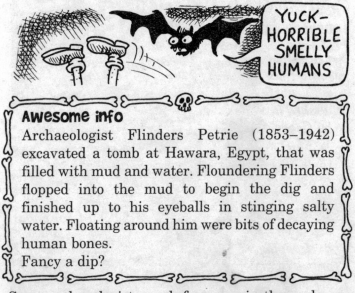

Awesome info

Archaeologist Flinders Petrie (1853–1942) excavated a tomb at Hawara, Egypt, that was filled with mud and water. Floundering Flinders flopped into the mud to begin the dig and finished up to his eyeballs in stinging salty water. Floating around him were bits of decaying human bones.

Fancy a dip?

Some archaeologists work for years in these places, laboriously clearing and sifting the rubble for tiny finds. And they often find that all the treasure and probably even the mummies were stolen years ago.

Obviously this work requires a tough breed of archaeologist. One of the first people to explore ancient tombs was one of the toughest imaginable...

It's tough at the tomb: Giovanni Belzoni (1778–1823)

Italian-born Giovanni was destined to cast a long shadow in archaeology – well, he was 2 metres (6 feet, 7 inches) tall in his socks. But his early life was nothing do with the past – he earned his living in circuses lifting 22 people at a time.

He went to Egypt to sell the government a water wheel to lift water. (It worked a bit like a hamster wheel with an ox instead of a hamster. Giovanni, of course, knew a thing or two about lifting.) But a test of the new machine ended in disaster when a boy broke his leg trying to prove that humans could do anything an ox could.

Anyway, a British diplomat paid Belzoni to lift a huge ancient statue and transport it to England. When he delivered the statue it must have been a weight off his mind (and no, he *didn't* carry it on his back). It was at this time that Belzoni met and fell out with his deadly rival Bernardino Drovetti (1776–1852). Their rivalry was so dramatic it would make a great Hollywood movie. Anyway, I've written the film script so I expect it won't be long now. Unlike most Hollywood blockbusters, all the facts in this film are *true*, but I might have made up some of the speeches.

Awesome Archaeology Productions presents...

AWESOME TOMB RAIDERS

An action-packed comedy-horror-thriller for all the family!

Awesome Tomb Raider Script

Scene 1: A ruin in Egypt (desert palm trees, lots of sand, etc.)

Belzoni is shouting to his workmen, who are moving a huge carved pharaoh's head.

B: Hey guys, put your backs into it – we can do it! Just wait till the folks back home see this!

Men: H-e-a-v-e, groan!

SINCE THIS IS HOLLYWOOD, THE HERO, BELZONI, WILL BE PLAYED BY A BIG STAR (THE REAL BELZONI HAD AN ITALIAN ACCENT).

(Enter Drovetti - you can tell he's a villain by his ridiculous moustache, black cape and generally villainous appearance.)

Drovetti: Curses! Eet looks lak I hev been foiled! I hed ma eye on ze head and zat Belzoni eez sending it back to England! I hev tried to stop Belzoni by bribing ze Egyptian officials to stop heem ... but I hev failed!

Belzoni: You won't stop me, Drovetti! I'm gonna find me some temples and clean up!

Drovetti: Zat eez what you theenk, Belzoni! (Gives a sinister laugh.)

Scene 2: The Temple of Karnak (lots of sand and ancient mummies lying around)
Subtitle on screen: The Temple of Karnak
(Enter Belzoni.)

Belzoni: Jeez look at them mighty fine ruins! They kinda make a guy feel small and insignificant!

Belzoni trips and falls heavily.

Belzoni: Ouch! I nearly bust my goddamn nose! Oh hail, I've sat on a mummy!

Belzoni: Say, this mummy dust sure gets up a fella's

nose. Lucky I ain't got no sense of smell! Atishoo! AGGGH, it's kinda sore!

(Enter Drovetti.)

Drovetti: What's theez, sitting around on ze job, Belzoni?

Belzoni: Hey no way, mister – I've excavated Abu Simbel temple and found the lost entrance to the lesser pyramid at Giza, so match that, wise guy!

Drovetti: I, er...

Belzoni: Yeah and now I'm gonner get me some valuable ancient Egyptian tomb treasure!

Scene 3: A tomb

(Belzoni is admiring the tomb paintings.)

Belzoni: This place sure is fit for a king!

Pity it's been robbed, but the paintings look real neat and this coffin case is humungous!

(Drovetti creeps into shot.)

Belzoni: Say, how ya doin', Drovetti – still up to your no-good thieving tricks?

Drovetti: Do not worry, Senior Belzoni. I will not try to steal anytheeng. You ken hev theez coffin case with ma bleseeng!

86

Drovetti: (aside) Ha ha, Belzoni will nat be able to move eet and he will look ze big fool!

Belzoni: Why thankee, kindly good buddy. Say, can I take that huge obelisk at Philae too?

Drovetti: Ha ha, if you weesh!

Scene 4: A road by the pyramids

(Drovetti is addressing a gang of sinister-looking bandits all of whom have moustaches.)

Drovetti: I hev schemed and plotted against Belzoni but nothing can stop heem! He hez taken the obelisk zat I thought could not be moved. Grrr, we must put ze frightners on heem!

(They quickly hide in bushes.)

(Enter Belzoni on a donkey.)

Belzoni: Gee up Dobbin! Yee-ha!

Donkey: Ee-aw!

(Drovetti and bandits leap out.)

Drovetti: You are feenished, Belzoni! Get off your donkey and face ze music.

Belzoni: Hey, what's going on? I ain't getting down for the likes of you, Drovetti! A gun goes off behind Belzoni. Belzoni quickly leaps off donkey.

Belzoni: OK, you win! I'm unarmed, so what's the deal?

Drovetti: You leev ze country and neevar return.

Belzoni: Sure thing, I'm outta here anyhow. But I'm not leaving without that coffin case I found!

Drovetti: Very well – move it if you can, ha ha!

Scene 5: The port

Belzoni's ship is setting sail. Belzoni is on deck with the coffin case.

Belzoni: Well, shifting that there coffin case was no big deal. It sure helps to be an expert weightlifter. Now I'm bound for England, fame and fortune!

(Cut to Drovetti on the shore hopping up and down with fury.)

Drovetti: Grr, foiled again!

(Cut to ship sailing into sunset, title, music, credits, THE END.)

SO WHAT HAPPENED NEXT?

You'll be pleased to hear that Belzoni staged a successful exhibition of his discoveries. And you'll be even more chuffed to know that the villainous Drovetti fell out with his friends and eventually went mad. But you won't be so happy to learn that Belzoni didn't earn a penny from the coffin case. Under a deal with the authorities in Egypt, they kept the first £2,000 – and the case sold for *exactly* £2,000!

And finally, you'll be absolutely gutted to discover that Belzoni died whilst exploring West Africa. On his grave was a note asking people to keep it tidy – but they didn't. Oh well, as Belzoni might have said, "that's show-business". (You're allowed to weep now, just so long as you don't blow your nose on this page.)

An important Point

As you may recall from page 12, before the days of systematic archaeology people who dug up old sites were treasure hunters and tomb robbers. And to be honest, Belzoni was simply a tomb robber who took an interest in the stuff he was robbing. Mind you, the Egyptians had been robbing tombs since ancient times.

Would you fancy being a tomb robber? If so, here's a handy book to help you. By the way, tomb robbers were a superstitious bunch and that's why this guide is based on folklore...

The Tomb Robber's Guide

Tomb robbing is an enjoyable and profitable hobby but you need to follow the rules or you'll be in dead trouble ...

Rule one

It's well known that evil spirits live inside ducks and that's why it's dangerous to follow a duck into a tomb. In the tomb the duck spirit can enter your body. If this happens you'd best duck out of the tomb and seek a quack doctor.

Rule two

Deadly scorpions live in tombs. If you get bitten, cut open the wound and suck out the poison. Next, drink a mixture of olive oil and crushed garlic (if you breathe on a flower and it wilts you'll know that you've chewed enough garlic).

Rule three

Tomb robbers in ancient Egypt were tortured by being beaten on the feet with rods and having a screw tightened on their bodies. Then they were stuck on pointed stakes and left to die. So tomb robbers, BEWARE – your life could be at stake.

← AVOID THESE

Rule four

Don't forget to say spells to ward off evil spirits or curses in the tomb. Oh, and talking about magic, here's a magic recipe to help you find treasure...

Mix up the incense and plants – saffron, figs and carob – and some dung, and moisten the mixture with human blood.

Roll into a pellet.

Set it on fire and you're bound to sniff out treasure (or sniff out something awful).

Important note
The scorpion-bite cure wasn't very helpful, but don't worry – scorpion bites are only fatal in old or very young people. So it's tough luck for your little brother/sister and your teacher – but you should be OK!

Most of the advice was taken from an old Egyptian book called the *Book of Buried Pearls*. The advice was so awesomely useless that in 1907 archaeologist Gaston Maspero (1846–1916) published the book cheaply so that tomb robbers would read it and *not* find any tombs to rob.

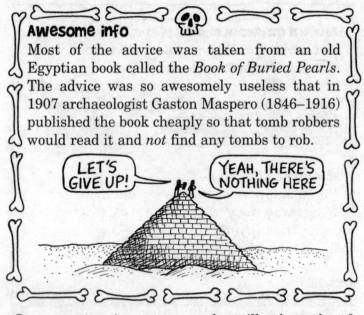

LET'S GIVE UP!

YEAH, THERE'S NOTHING HERE

On a more serious note, crooks still rob tombs of their treasures and sell them to rich and greedy collectors. (See page 124 for a story about a robber in the USA.) Theft from sites is a big and growing problem in many parts of the world. In 1987 archaeologist Walter Alva found a vast treasure in Sipan in Peru. A tomb robber told the police about the site after falling out with his fellow thieves. But by the time the archaeologists arrived the place was crawling with robbers and the police had to fight them off.

The case of the terrible tomb robber
Can you believe it – our pal Howard Carter once tracked down a tomb robber?! Here's what Carter's report might have looked like – would *you* have made the same decisions?

Howard Carter's Report

1907

Disaster! The tomb of Amenhotep II was broken into last night and the mummy partly unwrapped by a thief who was searching for jewellery. This is a grave crime...

1 So what did Carter do?
a) Check out news of other crimes in the area.
b) Booby-trap the mummy so it exploded next time someone tried to touch it.
c) Lie in wait for the thief's return.

Answer: a)

A neighbouring tomb had been rifled a few days before, so I decided to look there for clues to my robbery. Well, I found them, didn't I? The thief had broken the lock on the tomb door and tried to make the lock appear unbroken by using resin and small bits of lead. The same trick was used on Amenhotep's tomb. Clearly the same thief was involved in both crimes – he had to be a professional. I began searching for more clues.

Then I found footprints. They appeared to lead towards the house of Mohammed Abd el Rassoul. Well, that's suspicious. Everyone whispers that he's into tomb robbing...

2 What did Carter do?
a) Kick down the robber's door and accuse him of the crime.
b) Call the police.
c) Photograph and measure the footprints.

Answer: **c)** He wanted more proof of the robber's guilt.

I measured the prints and photographed them. My skills as an archaeologist came in handy here!) Next I hired an expert tracker to check that the trail really did lead to the thief's door. Well, the police picked up Mohammed but he denies everything. Luckily, I had my photos and measurements and the footprints fit his feet exactly! He looked really de-feeted when I told him!

Assuming that the tomb you're excavating hasn't been robbed, there's a strong possibility that you'll find a dead body inside. Well, by some revolting coincidence you'll find a dead body or two inside the next chapter. And you'll also discover what the best-dressed ancient bodies are wearing and what you might find in their festering *guts*.

Warning: The next pages aren't very tasteful ... unless you're a cannibal!

DEAD INTERESTING PEOPLE

Archaeologists think that ancient bodies are dead interesting. It might sound awesomely gruesome but the bodies can tell us a lot about how they lived ... and how they died.

And talking about ancient bodies, let's find out what's been happening at Killem School since our last visit. Remember how archaeologists discovered the remains of an old school? Well, you might also recall that they found a skull too, and the latest news is that they've found a skeleton to go with the skull and three *more* skeletons!

So let's go and bone up on the evidence...

The Dead School
Part 3: Body of evidence
"I'm not surprised you've found skeletons," said Samantha brightly. "That's what I was trying to say. According to this old newspaper I found, in 1790 there was an outbreak of disease at the school and three pupils died. Isn't that fab?"

Professor Helga Digby lent over to comfort Kevin who was pale and shaking after his encounter with the skull.

"Kevin, it's only a skull. You're supposed to be an archaeologist – you're supposed to be fascinated by them."

Kevin's teeth started chattering. "Well, y-y-yes I am, Prof, as long as they're only in b-b-b-ooks. In fact, my a-a-archaeology b-b-book has a chapter about bones..."

"Well then, Kevin," said the Professor kindly. "You'd best sit quietly and read it until you calm down. I'm sure we can excavate just fine without you."

Archaeology for Beginners by EC Peasy

Chapter Six: Bones for Beginners

Bones are brilliant! At least we archaeologists think so! You can tell so much about a person – like whether an adult's skeleton was a man or a woman.

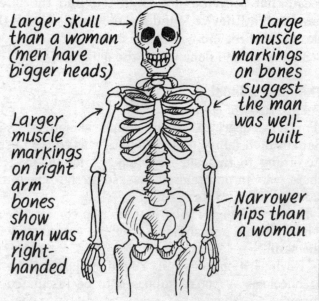

Skeleton of man

Larger skull than a woman (men have bigger heads)

Larger muscle markings on right arm bones show man was right-handed

Large muscle markings on bones suggest the man was well-built

Narrower hips than a woman

And you can work out a young person's age by their bones. As the body grows older the bone tips (separate in children) fuse with the rest of the bone.

"Hi, Kevin," said Samantha. "Are you *really* scared of skeletons?"

Kevin looked up from his book and blushed to the roots of his hair. "Not really," he mumbled.

"OK, then you can go and help Norman — he's really busy. I'll be back later — the Professor's asked me to ring the press and TV."

Kevin's eyes widened in panic. "Cor," he said weakly. "I've always wanted to be on telly."

97

Memo
From: Miss Meek, English Teacher
To: Mr Snipe, Head Teacher
I am afraid that the discovery of human remains might upset the more sensitive children. May I suggest that we bring in counsellors and close the school for a few weeks?

Memo
From: Mr Snipe, Head Teacher
To: Miss Meek
Re: Your memo - FORGET IT! Miss Meek, you are paid to teach, not to send children on holidays! If I had my way this so-called dig would never have happened - but it's too late to stop it.

Meanwhile at the playing field, the sensitive, delicate little children had come to see the skull...

Science Homework by Claire

DNA

DNA stands for deoxyribose nucleic acid - a substance found in body cells. According to the Education Channel Programme I videoed, the arrangement of chemicals in DNA controls how the body grows and develops. Related people have similar DNA and archaeologists can study DNA from old bones or teeth to find out if two bodies came from the same family.

A - Excellent work, as ever!

Meanwhile the archaeologists worked on, little knowing that they were about to uncover an *even more* horrifying secret...
To be continued...

At Killem School the bodies are simply skeletons and that's what archaeologists mainly find when they dig up old graveyards or battlefields.

But not always...

Awesome info

Archaeologists at Sutton Hoo, England, have found a complete cemetery where people were sacrificed over 1,000 years ago and buried in strange contorted positions. But all the bodies had dissolved and all that remained were ghostly shadows in the sand.

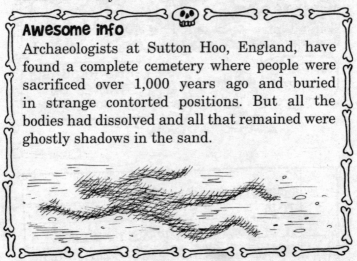

But sometimes, if an archaeologist is *really lucky* they might come across a body with a few tatters of rotting flesh or even something more. Are you ready for...

The horror in the Bog

No one in their right minds would visit a bog on holiday. They're damp and smelly and scary and often wrapped in mist. And the quaking ground can swallow a person in minutes and steep them in a germ-killing acid that ensures that their body doesn't rot. That's why bogs in Denmark, Germany, England, Florida and Ireland have yielded ancient bodies complete with bones, skin and guts. Some of the bodies had died violently. One German bog body had been chucked into the bog inside a barrel lined with nails (and I bet that *wasn't* a barrel of laughs).

Awesome info

Tollund man was found in 1950. He'd been hanged, then he hung around in a Danish bog for 2,000 years. Today you can see the man's preserved head in the National Museum, Copenhagen. The head needed a year of chemical treatment to preserve it, but during that time it shrank by 12 per cent.

And now for the sickening tale of how another bog body was discovered...

A BOG-STANDARD BODY

HULDREMOSEN, DENMARK, 1879 A MAN CUTTING PEAT REALIZED HE'D CUT OFF A HUMAN HAND WITH HIS SHARP SPADE. THEN HE FOUND THE REST OF THE BODY. IT WAS AN OLD WOMAN.

FOR PEAT'S SAKE, LOOK AT THIS!

A CROWD GATHERED BUT ONE OF THEM, A TEACHER (TRUST A TEACHER TO BE A KNOW-ALL) REALIZED THE BODY WAS VERY OLD.

THAT OLD WOMAN SHOULD BE PUT IN A MUSEUM!

YOU WATCH YOUR TONGUE, YOUNG MAN!

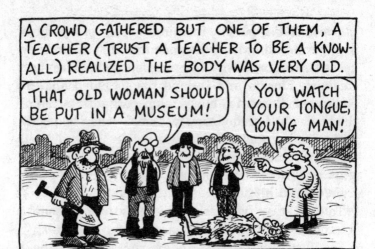

THEN THE POLICE ARRIVED.

DOES ANYONE NEED A HAND?

WE'VE ALREADY FOUND ONE

BEFORE THE OLD WOMAN DIED HER ARM HAD BEEN CUT OFF WITH AN AXE.

IF YOU ASK ME SHE'S QUITE 'ARMLESS

THE VILLAGERS PUT THE OLD WOMAN IN A COFFIN AND BURIED HER IN THE CHURCH-YARD. THEN THE MUSEUM ASKED FOR THE BODY TO BE SENT TO THEM FOR STUDY SO THE VILLAGERS HAD TO DIG IT UP AGAIN.

GRUNT! GROAN!

ODDLY ENOUGH, THE MUSEUM OFFICIALS PUT THE BODY IN A BASEMENT AND EXPERTS DIDN'T STUDY IT UNTIL 1978. THE BODY WAS FOUND TO DATE FROM AD 100.

Awesome info

There is an old superstition that if you take a body from the bog you must leave another to satisfy the gods. When archaeologists dug the body of Tollund Man from the bog a volunteer suffered a heart attack and died. Had the gods demanded another victim?

But bogs aren't the only way to preserve bodies – cold also kills the germs that cause rotting. That's why food stays fresh in your freezer, and so would a body if you put one in there...

FROZEN IN TIME

In 1991 archaeologists got a chance to study a frozen body even older than the bog bodies. It was found high in the Alps by hikers Erika and Helmut Simon. The body was quickly christened Otzi. Now in a WORLD EXCLUSIVE we've persuaded the ice-man to break his 5,300 year silence...

My story...
by Otzi the ice-man

hi there!

I should never have died like that. Stupid it was.
Mum said, "Stay off that mountain, son – you've not been well."
"Listen, mum," I said proudly. "I'm 45 – I'm a herdsman and it's my job."
"But it's not safe!" protested Mum.
"Course it is, mum. I've got all my own gear –

axe, bows, arows, knife, and I'll
wrap up warm I promise."
Yeah, I reckoned I could look
after myself all right. Silly me
- I should have listened to my
mum.
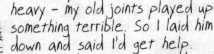

The other tribe have stolen
our sheep for years so when I caught them I
lost it. Well, it's easily done. There were three
of them. They went for us but we fought them
off. My hands bled but I got two with my arrows
and the other ran for it. Then I saw my mate
was hurt. I tried to carry him but he was too
heavy – my old joints played up
something terrible. So I laid him
down and said I'd get help.

I walked for a while and then
I sat and pondered what to do.
I never saw the warriors from
the other tribe until it was too
late. They'd come after me. As I leapt to my
feet an arrow smashed into my shoulder. Then I
fell and bashed my head...

Next thing I knew the snow that covered me
melted and I heard these hikers talking.

"But it's a man!" a woman was
saying.

Of course I am - I should
know.
"You're wrong," said a man. "It's
a piece of rubbish!"

cheek! Well, for a time I had no peace. There were police and mountain rescue people everywhere. They used ice-picks and some kind of machine chisel to dig me out of the ice. Then they bust me hip and broke my arm forcing me into a coffin – ouch! And now I'm stuck in a freezer to stop me rotting and they only allow me out for 15 minutes every fortnight – the whole thing just leaves me cold.

FREEZER

What a rotten life! Er, I mean death.

Archaeological notes

1 The brilliant thing about Otzi is that he was found with all his belongings around him (a bit different to being buried with things that people thought he might need in the afterlife). Normally in archaeology such personal things get thrown away and muddled up with other people's belongings so you can't really discover who owned what.

2 Otzi's story is based on facts discovered by archaeologists. We know he made his belongings because they carry marks made by his tools.

3 Otzi was studied by Austrian archaeologists but his body was actually found just inside Italy. This caused arguments between the two countries over who owned the frozen bod. In the end Otzi went to Italy.

Actually, Otzi isn't the only ancient corpse that became a post-mortem celebrity. There are quite a few and did you know they've got their own celebrity magazine?

Well, they have!

Fashion and beauty with Katie Cadaver
Ice-cool fashions

Otzi is modelling the latest Bronze Age fashions. This season fur and leather is the in thing and no body should be seen dead without it...

For everyday wear, hand-spun wool is definitely in. Annifried is modelling the designer dress worn by a 3,000-year-old Danish girl found in an oak coffin.

FUR CAP

SHEEP FUR COAT

LEATHER LOINCLOTH

FUR LEGGINGS

COW SKIN SHOES FILLED WITH GRASS

ONE-PIECE THIGH LENGTH WOOLLEN DRESS

Clothes Supplied by BODS-R-US

Important note

When it was discovered in 1921 the dress shocked archaeologists. They thought it was rude because it showed the girl's legs. They were less shocked by the fact that nothing remained of the girl's head except her brain and her eyebrows.

Katie's beauty tips

This week: Super skin and natural nails

Cold winds can make your skin terribly dry and wrinkled, especially after the first thousand years. Why not try a mud-pack as used by the people of ancient Chile on mummies (6000 BC). Simply smoke your body like a kipper and cover your face and any other bits you want to preserve in mud.

Flaky fingernails and bad hair days

Burial in ice can be a killer for your fingernails. Poor Otzi's hair and nails actually dropped off, but fortunately some nice archaeologists climbed the mountain and found most of his hair and one of his nails.

HORROR-SCOPES
by Mary Moulder

August

You will be in a glass display case this month. Many people will come to stare at you and say things like "Cor, it's better than the chamber of horrors!" or "Yuck! Look at those fingernails!"

Health with Dr Bonaparte Skullbones

Dear Doc,
I'm a boy from the Inca people of South America. My body's been up a mountain for five hundred years after I was sacrificed to the gods. My problem is that scientists have found that I've got warts – is it catching?
Worried, South America

Dear Worried,
Don't worry, since you've been dead for so long the germs that caused the ailment are probably dead too.
PS Thanks for the postcard of your tomb – the view looks lovely!

ANY BODY OUT THERE?

Lonely mummy (own tomb) seeks soul-mate for eternity. I'm 3,300 years old and not too well preserved but I'll let you drive my chariot.

Contact Tut, c/o Valley of the Kings.

Dear Doc,

I'm a 600-year-old Inca mummy from Peru. A team of Italian and Argentinean scientists and archaeologists have said I had Chagas' disease. I'm really worried – am I going to die?
Sickly, Peru

Dear Sickly,

You can't die because you're already dead, remember? The disease was caused by bugs sucking your blood and then poo-ing in the wound. The deadly droppings contained a microscopic bug that stopped your guts working. Your poo built up making your guts swell and then your heart stopped beating. It must have been a fascinating way to go!

Cookery with Daphne Deadbody

Some people might find this hard to digest but we dead people love our food. Yes, mummy's cooking is definitely best! This month all our recipes are based on the preserved stomach contents of dead people. Bon appetit!

Starters
Delicious fresh water melon

Ingredients
One water melon

You need the exact type as eaten by the Marchioness of Dai, a Chinese lady. She ate the melon and Dai-ed one hour later of a heart attack.

Method
1 Cut into cubes and serve with yoghurt. Eat and allow to digest for one hour – it's good for your guts!
2 Allow to remain in the stomach for 2,200 years.
Griddle cake
As eaten by Pete Marsh (the body found in Lindow Moss, England, in 1984).
Ingredients
Coarsely ground flour
Water

Method

1 Mix the flour and water and bake over a hot iron until cooked.

2 Eat and 12 hours later get yourself brutally done to death.

3 Steep well in acid bog water (for around 2,000 years).

Problem page with Dee Kay

Dear Dee,
Two thousand years ago someone kneed me in the ribs and hit me from behind with an axe to knock me out. Then they strangled me and slit my throat so my blood drained out and dumped me in a bog. Do I bring out the worst in people?
Pete Marsh
British Museum, London.

Dear Pete,
Of course not, Pete. People love seeing you in your glass case. The people who attacked you liked you too – they just thought that it would be nice to sacrifice you to the gods. I know it's tough but we've all got to make sacrifices sometimes.

NEXT MONTH: CELEBRITY CORPSES INVITE US TO TAKE A LOOK AROUND THEIR LOVELY TOMBS

Pete Marsh was found after a worker at a local peat packing factory found what he thought was a stick and threw it at a workmate. The stick was a human leg with a foot attached. So what would YOU do, leg it? Pete's other leg and foot had already been packed up as peat fertilizer and used to grow mushrooms. I expect they gave a nice flavour to mushroom soup.

Actually, throwing away bits of ancient body is a big mistake because even a tiny bit of body (and not necessarily the stomach) can tell archaeologists what an ancient person *ate* … it's true.

DUG-UP DETAILS

Name: Chemicals, diet and dead bodies.
The basic facts:

Remember carbon-14 dating? (It's on page 51 if you can't.) Well, there are other types of carbon atom that build up in bones.

SLIGHTLY DIFFERENT

The detailed bits:

You get more carbon-13 in sea food and carbon-12 is higher in plants. So you take a sample of bone and count up the types of carbon atoms using a machine called a mass spectrometer. You can then work out what your dead person has been eating. Er, wouldn't it be easier to ask them?

Teeth truths

If you're not bothered about fingering dead people's bones then you'll probably be happy to peer in their mouldering mouths and take a look at their *teeth*.

Open wide now...

1 In Japan, between 2,000 and 4,000 years ago, it was fashionable to knock out some of your teeth when you got to 14. The particular teeth you had pulled out depended on which area you came from.

YOU'RE NOT FROM ROUND HERE, ARE YOU?

2 Israeli archaeologists found a 2,000-year-old warrior's skull with a green tooth. A dodgy dentist must have promised to give the man a gold filling but gave him a bronze one instead. The poisonous bronze probably killed the warrior and turned green in a chemical reaction. I expect the warrior turned green after he died too.

SAY AAAARGH!

3 You've seen the famous painting of the Mona Lisa with her mysterious smile? If not, here's a version our awesome artist knocked up in his tea-break...

The lady in the painting is thought to be Isabella of Naples (1470–1524) but she's now known as Lisa del Giocondo. Well, that was lucky. Archaeologists who found Isabella's skull discovered that she had black teeth with their enamel scraped off – so she wouldn't have smiled so nicely.

4 You can find out how old someone is by studying their teeth. The roots of the teeth become see-through with age – perhaps your teacher would allow you study her teeth to find out if she's as young as she claims to be.

5 Marks on the teeth may show whether the person ate meat or was vegetarian, and generally what sort of diet they ate. Worn teeth mean that the food was tough and full of grit. Teeth can even tell you about a person's table manners, or lack of them...

Do it yourself ... eat like a Cave Person

Do your parents tell you that you eat like a cave person? Now's your chance to prove them right!

All you need is...

A stringy strip of meat (anything will do, try ham, dead mammoth, or, if you're a vegetarian, you could try dead spinach).

A flint knife (or you could use an ordinary blunt knife).

All you do is...

1 Hold one end of the meat in your front teeth and the other end in your hand.

2 Cut the meat with your knife.

3 Gulp down the bit of food that's hanging down from your mouth without dropping it on the floor.

Archaeologists have found marks on the teeth of 500,000-year-old skulls suggesting that this is how cave people ate. Messy, eh?

Awesome info

Ancient people had larger jaws than people today. Not surprising really. Before modern stoves, food was poorly cooked and tougher – so it needed more chewing. And before forks were invented in the 1600s it was harder for people to cut up their food so they chewed it instead. Mind you, children reared on rubbery school dinners should have jaws like King Kong.

SPOT THE DIFFERENCE

Have you got the guts to read this Bit?

Most preserved bodies suffered from gut worms. The worm eggs plopped out in poo and could be transported to food on dirty hands. Once in the body they hatched into more worms. No, DON'T PANIC, you almost certainly don't have any and even if you did they're easily treated. By the way, some Egyptian mummies contain maw-worms – this creature grows to 30 cm (1 foot) and enjoys exploring the body. It sometimes pops out of the little pink corners next to the eyeballs. Maw pudding anyone?

But talking about food, did you know that bits of rotting, half-eaten food are fascinating finds because they tell archaeologists about the diet of early people? And there's one type of find that's even more interesting – dried-up poo.

What else will you find in the next chapter?

117

FASCINATING FINDS

Archaeology is garbage. Yes, you did read that right, most finds – the objects that archaeologists discover – are *rubbish*! Useless trash like animal bones and broken pottery that people threw away in tips called middens. Archaeologists sieve through middens and get a true picture of what life was really like.

Could you Be an arChaeologist?

US archaeologist William L Rathje studied modern rubbish to see if it can tell us about the way *we* live. A team of archaeologists interviewed people in Tucson, Arizona and trawled their rotting garbage. 85 per cent of people said they *didn't* drink beer – but what did the archaeologists discover?

a) The people were telling the truth.

b) Only 25 per cent *didn't* drink beer – the others had beer cans in their rubbish.

c) The archaeologists got drunk on beer and lost their survey results.

Anyway, now for some slightly older finds ...

A Curious Cabinet

Four hundred years ago, before there were museums, rich people used to collect ancient objects and display them in a special case called a "cabinet of curiosities".

Why not set up your own cabinet?

You could display...

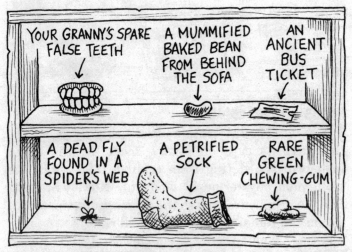

YOUR GRANNY'S SPARE FALSE TEETH

A MUMMIFIED BAKED BEAN FROM BEHIND THE SOFA

AN ANCIENT BUS TICKET

A DEAD FLY FOUND IN A SPIDER'S WEB

A PETRIFIED SOCK

RARE GREEN CHEWING-GUM

You'll be interested to know that we've assembled a cabinet of curiosities for this book. They're archaeological finds taken from museums all over the world. They've been selected not for their value but because each one tells a story. But you'd better take a look at it now before the museums start demanding their property back. (Oops!)

119

1. A DEAD FLY FROM A VIKING SETTLEMENT IN GREENLAND

2. ELEVEN SCRAPS OF POTTERY WITH NAMES ON THEM FROM THE FORTRESS OF MASADA IN ISRAEL

3. A CHUNK OF ROMAN WALL FROM POMPEII, ITALY

4. AN ANCIENT TABLET FROM UR, IRAQ

5. A LUMP OF FOSSILIZED POO FROM SOUTH-WEST USA

Notes on the objects

1 Not terribly interesting? Well, this fly is a type that lays its eggs on rotting meat. It was found in a bedroom dating from around 1350 when the settlement mysteriously died out. Now, you don't find meat in bedrooms, so the fly maggots must have fed on the remains of a rotting Viking!

2 Boring? Well, in AD 73, 1,000 Jewish fighters held a Roman army at bay at Masada. The people killed one another rather than give up and the last 11 survivors chose one man to kill the others before killing himself. The selection was made by lot – so could

120

these fragments be the remains of that fatal raffle?

3 Boring? Hardly! Walls in Pompeii had more graffiti than a school toilet. There were ads and messages like "Potumnus loves Apliandra", and rude Roman jokes (no, I'm not going to repeat these because boring adults will try to ban this book) and this poem written by an anti-graffiti graffiti artist:

I WONDER, WALL –
THAT YOU DON'T GO SMASH
WHEN YOU BEAR THE WEIGHT
OF ALL THIS TRASH!

Poetry like this is enough to drive you up the wall!

4 Tablets were pieces of clay on which people wrote, remember? This one has a 3,000-year-old account of a school day. Here's a rough translation:

I HAD TO RUN TO SCHOOL BECAUSE I'D GET BEATEN IF I WAS LATE. I HAD TO RECITE STUFF LEARNT FROM A TABLET AND THEN WE GOT LOADS MORE WORK. I GOT BEATEN FOR TALKING, BEATEN FOR STANDING UP AND BEATEN FOR BAD HANDWRITING. I HATE SCHOOL!

Sounds familiar? (I made up the last three words but the rest of the translation is TRUE!)

5 Revolting? You bet – and it hides a more horrible secret. The poo was found at a site occupied by the Anasazi people in about 1150. It was found close to a pile of human bones that looked as if they'd been cooked for meat. So were the Anasazi cannibals? A test of the poo revealed chemicals found only in human meat so perhaps they had a guest for lunch…

Ask an archaeologist

NAME TWO COUNTRIES THAT HAVE ARCHAEOLOGICAL FINDS ON THEIR FLAGS

GASP!

You can award the archaeologist a mark each for the country and two bonus marks if they can name the finds and the sites where they came from (fat chance, ha ha).

Answer:

1 Zimbabwe. The country is named after Great Zimbabwe, a ruined palace built by the local Shona people in 1270. The flag of Zimbabwe features a carved stone bird found near by.

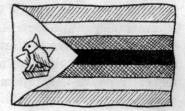

2 Macedonia. The flag was inspired by the star found on a gold box. The box contained the burnt bones of a man believed to be  Philip II (382–336 BC) King of Macedonia and the dad of megastar-conqueror Alexander the Great. The flag annoys many Greeks because Philip's ancient Kingdom of Macedonia was actually in Greece and the gold box was found there.

But meanwhile some greedy people are still prepared to pay for stolen ancient treasures. And robbers are still raiding archaeological sites and selling the objects they find. Here's a story about a man who made a living doing just that...

The Story of Richard Wetherill

by his devoted servant and sidekick
Hiram Firem

When Richard was just a boy him and his four brothers loved exploring. They was for ever riding into the sunset. Them boys was real close - like brothers they was. Why, heck I'm forgetting - they was brothers!

Richard loved collecting old Indian pottery from local ruins and pretty soon folks started to drop by the Wetherill homestead just to see what he'd picked up. I guess that gave Richard the idea of showing off his finds. His big break came back in 1888 when he found the cliff palace in Mesa Verde. It was just a pile of ruins but to Richard it really was a palace. He spent hours digging up pottery there and reckoned he could make a pile of bucks by exhibiting it back in Denver.

Well, he didn't ('scuse me whilst I spit out this quid of chewing baccy). He near enough bankrupted himself! But just when things hit rock bottom his cousin sent him a mummy. Now that mummy was just a dried-up old body and it wasn't much to look at with its crumbling skin and ugly wrinkled face, but folks came from far and wide just to stare at it. So Richard made his big bucks and he spent all his time up at the Mesa - why he even opened a store to sell that there pottery.

A BUNCH OF OLD POTS AN' A MUMMY

But eventually them big-shot politicians in Washington figured that they'd had enough of folks digging up ancient pots and they put a stop to it. ('Scuse me whilst I have a good ole splutter.) Richard took up farming but I'm truly sorry to say he was gunned down by a cattle raider back in 1910. Well, folks is different now and we know it ain't right to raid old sites any more than it was right for that there robber to blow away my best friend.

Today archaeologists make more finds than ever. That's because nowadays they carefully sieve the soil for tiny finds (remember those bits of beetle and pollen from page 33?) and they don't miss a thing. For example, archaeologists working at Meadowcroft, a Stone Age site in Pennsylvania, USA, sorted 2.5 *million* tiny finds – it was a big job but they got it sorted, ha ha. Here's a method of removing tiny finds from soil that you might like to try...

Do it yourself ... sieving for secrets

All you need...

- 2–3 trowelfuls of earth in a bucket (and don't even think of bringing them indoors – this activity is strictly for outdoors).
- An old tea strainer
- A bucket of water
- Gardening gloves
- Some seeds (sesame seeds will do).

All you do is...

1 Put on the gardening gloves before handling earth.

2 Mix the seeds with the earth.

3 Add water so it covers the earth by 5 cm (2 inches). Swill the mixture around.

What happens?

Answer: The seeds and tiny archaeological finds, such as slivers of bone, fish scales, ants' contact lenses, etc. will float and you can remove them with the strainer. This technique was developed by archaeologist Stuart Struever working at Illinois in the 1970s. The original technique also involved standing in the river and operating a huge sieve – but you're excused that bit...

LOST LANGUAGES

Ancient people wrote in ancient languages that are mostly long since forgotten. So, to read their words archaeologists have had to re-learn the languages.

But how can they do this? Find a really ancient teacher? Chances are that not even your language teacher is that old!

No, it's done through careful detective work and a few inspired guesses. The first language to be deciphered was ancient Egyptian. In 1798, a French soldier found an ancient stone near Rosetta, Egypt, inscribed with a text in Greek and ancient Egyptian. Scholars can read Greek and so it should have been straightforward to work out what the Egyptian writing said.

It wasn't.

It took Frenchman Jean Champollion (1790–1832) 15 years to link the symbols to the Greek words. And Champollion was a genius who could speak eight languages at the age of 17 – so it would have taken a normal person about 500 years. At last, Champollion found himself reading the name of Egyptian king Ramases. He was so excited that he rushed to see his brother, shouting, "I've got it!" Then he fainted.

Can You Crack the Maya Code?

More recently, archaeologists have decoded the script used by the ancient Maya people of Central America. Here there were no helpful texts in other languages for archaeologists to study and yet they made the key breakthrough in just *one day*. Could you do this?

Read on and find out!

In 1863 French scholar Brasseur de Bourbourg found a mysterious old book in Madrid. It was an account by a Spanish bishop of the Maya people. The bishop had spoken to some of the surviving Maya and written down their numbers and alphabet. Some of the signs were easy to make sense of.

1 What do these mean?

.

..

...

Clue: I'm counting on you to get them right!

In the 1950s, Russians Yuri Knosorov and Tatiana Proskouriakoff studied the strange letters. Yuri reckoned the letter signs were phonetic. No, that's nothing to do with a *telephone*, it's a posh word that means each symbol represents a sound in the spoken language. Tatiana guessed that these signs referred to dates in Mayan history and the inscriptions were recording the deeds of Mayan rulers.

One day in 1973, a small group of experts gathered in the ancient Mayan city of Palenque. They spread a copy of an inscription on a table and began to study it.

2 Assuming that Tatiana was right what two words or sets of words would you expect to appear lots of times...

KING   TOILET   CUSTARD   CROWN

PEANUTS BEAT/FOUGHT/KILLED (AND OTHER "DOING" WORDS)

Answers: 1 They're our numbers – 1, 2, 3. Actually, the numbers referred to years in the Mayan calendar.
2 KING and the "doing" words (the posh term for these is verbs).

The experts had cracked the Mayan code and found themselves reading huge chunks of Mayan inscriptions. And awesomely gory they were too! They often described brutal battles and savage human sacrifices to the gods.

I LOVE READING A GOOD HORROR STORY!

129

Wooden Writing

Archaeologists have even found private letters that prove that in some areas ordinary people could read and write. Hundreds of 800-year-old letters on pieces of bark found in Novgorod, Russia, have helped experts to discover the old Russian language spoken at the time. At the Vindolanda fort in northern England they've unearthed Roman letters written on fragile bark strips – amongst the texts found was a child's homework and a teacher's comment that it was sloppy work. Some things never change!

COULD DO BETTER, BOY!

SORRY SIR, MY ATTENTION KEEPS "ROMAN"

Roman teachers beat children, but let's hope that this teacher's *bark* was worse than his bite.

The bark strips are very fragile. The writing quickly fades when exposed to air and needs special chemical treatment. But that's typical of many finds as you can see in the next story...

WARNING: There's a mummy just about to be unwrapped in the next paragraph and the results are going to be awesomely messy. So put on some old clothes and a gas mask before you start reading...

Oh mummy, what a mess!

In 1907, archaeologist Theodore Davis found a lost tomb in the Valley of the Kings and important officials came to see the tomb opened.

First in was Joseph Lindon Smith, an artist who was employed to paint archaeological scenes. The tomb bore the name of Tutankhamun's granny (no, not his mummy)...

Joseph found that part of the ceiling had collapsed and rainwater had dripped through the roof. Luckily the mummy seemed OK.

A few days later the officials reassembled to watch the mummy being unwrapped by Joseph. The mummy was enclosed in thin sheets of pure gold...

Beneath the gold, the mummy was wrapped in bandages of frail, faded linen with golden bracelets on its wrists. Smith groped under the bandages for more jewellery.

Suddenly the mummy crumbled into dust: even the bones collapsed and in seconds all that was left were a few decayed bones and bits of skin. Oh, and some fragments of beautiful jewellery.

Archaeological notes

1 You'll be pleased to know that modern archaeologists don't often unwrap mummies. Nowadays they prefer to X-ray the bodies and insert special viewing tubes called endoscopes to look inside whilst doing as little damage as possible.

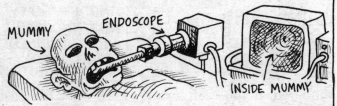

2 Most experts think the mummy was actually Tutankhamun's brother Smenkare. Obviously this is a terrible thing to happen to your brother. (I'm sure you'll agree!) This story highlights the fragility of some finds and the damage that unskilled people can do.

Fiendishly fragile finds

1 Photographer Harry Burton was taking a picture of a beautiful wooden statue of a girl found in an Egyptian tomb. Unfortunately, the tomb had been attacked by wood-eating bugs called termites and they had munched the statue until it was riddled with holes inside. When Burton took the picture the statue turned to dust. Luckily the picture came out fine.

2 King Tut's clothes appeared in good condition until someone touched them and they fell apart. Worse still, the clothes contained thousands of beads and sequins – one robe had 50,000 of them. And they all had to be sewn on to replicas.

Mind you, if you really want to see what the past was like, the best thing to do is to *reconstruct* it. That's to say, use ancient tools to make copies of things you found through archaeology. You can see what the past was like, hear and taste what the past was like, and even *smell* what it ponged like.

Why not take a sniff at the next chapter?

REVEALING RECONSRUCTIONS

These days, archaeologists do more than dig up the past. Action-seeking hardy souls that they are, they want to find out how ancient people actually *made* things. It's called "experimental archaeology" and some archaeologists have developed some really unusual skills. There'll be more about reconstructions after this commercial break…

DOING THINGS THE OLD WAY?

Archaeologists have done themselves injuries trying to move stones using methods available to ancient people. They have built walls at 500-year-old sites in South America using just shaped stones and no cement, and raised stones in ways that the builders of Stonehenge might have used. The only problem with these experiments is that there's usually no proof that ancient people actually did it this way.

AND I'VE DISCOVERED THEY MUST HAVE DONE THEIR BACKS IN!

Fantastic farming

In the 1970s archaeologists in Hampshire built a replica 2,000-year-old farm settlement. They found that Iron Age houses used 200 trees but were very strong. When they tried Iron Age farming they found that the types of wheat grown in the Iron Age grew very well.

At the end of the 1970s a group of volunteers lived in another replica Iron Age settlement for a whole year. They gave up central heating and cars and electric light and telephones and shopping in supermarkets and mostly enjoyed it. So maybe your granny's right: those were the good ol' days (actually she may not mean the Iron Age because she's not 2,000 years old).

Awesome info...

1 Reconstructed ancient farming methods often prove more successful than modern methods. In Bolivia, South American archaeologists have shown local people how to use the raised fields unused since 1450 to grow potatoes. The fields suffer less frost damage than ordinary fields and grow more spuds.

2 Israeli scientists have used ancient field systems to grow fruit in the desert. The fields collect water from a wide area and work well even in dry conditions.

Show-off Ships

Archaeologists have built and even sailed copies of ancient ships. For example, Thor Heyerdahl and Tim Severin made voyages to show that ancient people could cross the oceans. In 1947, Thor Heyerdhal sailed a raft 6,900 km (4,300 miles) to Rapa Nui (Easter Island) from South America to show how people might have reached the island. (Archaeologists now think the islanders made the shorter trip from Melanesia so Thor's theory must have had more holes than his raft.)

I'VE GOT A THOR STOMACH

More than 50 replicas of Viking ships have been built and sailed between places as far apart as Scandinavia and the USA. In the 1990s an intrepid group of Russian researchers built a replica Viking ship and took it down the Russian rivers from Smolensk to the Black Sea, following a Viking trade route. Meanwhile, an equally brave group of

Swedish researchers took their replica through a more northerly region of Russian rivers. Here's a letter that one of them might have written...

mud ↓

me

Somewhere on either the
Lovat or Dnieper rivers
Russia

Dear Mum,
Here I am cruising down the river. I feel like a real Viking, especially when I take a turn at the oars! Trouble is, every so often we get to rapids and have to pull the ship overland on a replica Viking cart - and our speed's not too rapid. I have to pull at the yoke (that's no yoke I can tell you!). And we keep getting attacked by mosquitoes and wasps. Who'd want to be a Viking?
Glad you're not here!

wasps

Love Lars

mosquitoes
more mud →

Could you be an archaeologist?

Here are accounts of five reconstructions. Can you predict what happened to the archaeologists?

1 Archaeologists in Iran found the oldest beer in the world or at least traces of the 5,000-year-old drink at the bottom of a jar. They decided to make their own ancient beer using a recipe dating from 1800 BC. The archaeologists served it to a group of US brewers. What happened?

a) The beer tasted awful and three of the brewers were sick on the carpet.

b) The beer was so strong everyone got drunk and there were embarrassing scenes that are best forgotten.

c) The beer was delicious!

2 Archaeologists are fascinated by food remains in the guts of dead bodies. (Maybe they find it hard to work on an empty stomach?) Appearing on TV, archaeologists Mortimer Wheeler and Glyn Daniel ate a gruel recipe based on the stomach contents of a 2,000-year-old body. What happened?

a) Both the archaeologists asked for a second helping.

b) The archaeologists were rushed to hospital with food poisoning.

c) The gruel tasted disgusting but the archaeologists just managed to keep it down.

3 In 1976 archaeologists built a replica fishing canoe of the Chumash people of California. Like the Chumash people, the archaeologists used stone tools and shark skin to smooth the wood. What happened?

a) The canoe sank.

b) The canoe leaked badly but it sailed quite well.

c) The archaeologists were blown off course and eventually reached Australia.

4 Archaeologist John Coles and a colleague fought a battle armed with replica swords and spears from 3,500 years ago. What happened?

a) One of the archaeologists was killed.

b) The battle seemed to prove that bronze shields were less useful for fighting than leather shields.

c) The police were called and both archaeologists were arrested.

5 Archaeologist George Frison threw a stone-tipped spear (based on those made 10,000 years ago by the Clovis people of North America) at a dead elephant. What happened?

a) The spear went through the elephant's tough skin.

b) The spear bounced off the elephant (it was designed for use on rabbits).

c) The elephant was actually alive (and having a snooze). The enraged jumbo chased the archaeologist half a mile.

Answers:

1 c) Scientists have develpoed sensitive tests for food traces so expect more ancient food and drink on the menu.

2 c) The gruel was made from crushed barley, linseed and seeds from several weeds (the bits of sand and moss also found in the original were left out) but it was still vile-tasting. The archaeologists had to swig brandy from a cow horn to wash it down.

3 b) The archaeologists got soaked and they had to bail out the canoe with a shell. But actually the *original* canoes leaked – so this was quite realistic. What's more, many people drowned when their canoes sank so if the canoe *had* sunk that would also have been authentic too.

4 b) The soft leather shield carried by John Coles was brilliant at soaking up sword cuts but the metal shield was cut to pieces. This suggests that bronze shields were made for show rather than use.

5 a) The spear could be used 12 times without damage (to the spear that is – the elephant was a bit more damaged, of course). Jumbo steak anyone?

But talking about hunting, can you believe that there was a real Stone Age hunter roaming California, USA, as recently as 1911 – the same era as early planes and Hollywood films? And can you also believe that the hunter showed archaeologists his way of life? Well, it's TRUE. And here's how one of the researchers might have told the story…

The last of the Yahi

Berkeley, September 1911

Dear Mary,
I am writing to let you know that I got back OK from Oroville. It really was a most strange experience. When we got to the town everyone was talking about the "wild man" the sheriff had caught and locked up in the jail. Well, the sheriff looked kind of surly when we dropped by.

"We're from the University of California," I said, "and we'd like to meet the man you captured. We believe he is the last survivor of the Yahi people."

"Darned if I care!" he spat. "That there savage is more trouble than he's worth."

me (taken aback)

the Sheriff

I was somewhat taken aback by this uncivil greeting and I replied, "Well, you can't keep him locked up for ever. It's not as if being a Stone Age hunter is a Federal offence."

I followed the sheriff into the jail where we saw the most miserable specimen of humanity I have ever set eyes on. He was exhausted and so thin his ribs stuck out. His cheeks were hollow and his close-set eyes were dark with fear.

"No one can get through to him," said the sheriff, reaching for his whisky bottle. "He speaks some kind of savage injun tongue no one's ever heard before."

Well, Mary, I spent the next few days trying to talk to the man using the books of native language I'd brought with me. But it was slow work and it's been decided that the man is coming back with us to the University Museum and that's where he'll live.

Well, I guess that's my news for now.

Your loving brother,

Thomas

Berkeley, March 1914

Dear Mary,

Thanks for your last letter. You wanted to know all about Ishi - that's what we're calling the wild man - so here's the latest. Ishi's doing just fine - he's settled into the museum and he shows visiting schoolkids how to make stone tools and arrowheads. He must be the last guy in America who has Stone Age skills. Now me and a few friends are planning to take Ishi back to his homeland and learn how to live like Stone Age people.

I'll let you know how it goes.

Your loving brother,

Thomas

Where are we? May 1914

Dear Mary,

Sorry about the soot stains - I'm writing this by the camp-fire. Living with Ishi is a real education. Did you know that a bow must season for weeks before it's right to use? Or that Stone Age hunters stalk animals for hours but often catch nothing? I should know - we were starving for two days before Ishi shot us a deer. We had to give up smoking because Ishi says the wild beasts can smell the tobacco, but he's right and without him we'd have died.

That Ishi is a real resourceful guy!

Your loving but rather hungry brother,

Thomas

Berkeley, August 1914

Dear Mary,

Just a quick postscript to my letter from the wilds. We're all safely back and for me it wasn't a moment too soon. I wasn't too sorry to sleep in a soft bed again with a hot dinner that I didn't have to remove guts from. But what an experience!

Ishi showed us the burial sites of his people. He showed us over 200 plants and herbs you can eat or use for medicine. Mary, I've been thinking it over – that sheriff was wrong! This man is no savage – he knows skills that the rest of the human race has forgotten and that makes him kind of special.

Write soon!

Your loving brother, *Thomas*

PS Come round to supper when you're in town. I cook a mean deer steak.

Oh well, that's enough about how archaeologists reconstruct the past – now it's your turn. Yes, *your* turn to try your hand at a bit of reconstruction! I hope you're ready for this...

Do it yourself ... make your own mummy

Remember the archaeologist on page 24 who made a mummy? Now it's your turn!

READ THIS BEFORE YOU START!
You'll need a dead body (of course). You *could* use your little brother/sister/teacher (as long as you don't mind being locked up for a very long time). Alternatively, you could use an old doll or teddy and go straight to step 5.

1 Prop up one end of a large table by placing books under the legs. This will allow the blood and brain juices to run down one end. (Remember to put lots of newspaper down and clear away the tea things first.) Lay the body on the table with the head at the upper end.

2 Stick a piece of wire up the nostrils of the body and into the brain. Whisk the wire round until the brain turns to a sort of porridge and slops out the nostrils. Chuck this away – your mummy doesn't need a brain. Pour some hot resin or pitch through the nostrils and into the skull instead. (This kills germs and prevents any bits of flesh left inside the skull from rotting.)

POKE, POKE

3 Cut open the body and whip out the stomach, guts, liver and kidneys. Slop these in special boxes. Leave the heart in place – as every ancient Egyptian knows, that's the bit you actually *think* with.

4 Pack the body with a mixture of salt and baking soda to dry it out. Leave in place for 35 days, then clean out the body and pour in more pitch.

5 Wrap the body in linen bandages. You could use strips of toilet paper – it's cheaper.

6 Place in a tomb for 3,000 years.

7 Sit down to a lovely picnic outside the tomb and break the cups and plates afterwards. Be careful – you might upset your mummy!

SORRY MUM, IT'S AN ANCIENT EGYPTIAN CUSTOM

That was the theory – but the practice was often very different. Some mummy-makers were awesomely AWFUL!

- A boy's mummy had its legs broken off to fit in a coffin.
- A female mummy was found with someone else's skull between her legs.
- Another mummy had its arms and legs muddled up and a stick to stop its head falling off.
- The mummy of King Amenhotep III had all its muscles pulled out and replaced with sawdust and mud. Unfortunately the skin split, with unhygienic results.

- One child's coffin was found to contain a mummified cat. The useless embalmers must have lost the body, *so they mummified their pet cat instead*!

Even King Tut's body was so badly preserved it would have lasted better if it had simply been buried in the dry desert sands.

Awesome info

In the Middle Ages, dealers in Egypt sold pitch scooped up from the innards of mummies as a medicine. Then people thought that if the pitch was good for you, so too was powdered mummy! Soon ships were exporting tons of mummified body bits to Europe for sick people to eat! French King Francis I (1494–1547) used to carry around a lump of ancient flesh to munch when he felt queasy. Sounds like a sick choke – er, joke to me.

I WANT MY MUMMY!

However, the good news is that even if the flesh has completely rotted away from a skull an expert can reconstruct that person's appearance. And now it's time to go over to Killem School where the archaeologists are about to use this technique. Yes, they've found skeletons at the site of the old school – remember? And now they want to know what one of them looked like...

The Dead School

Part 4: Let's face it!

Oswald wasn't happy. "Claire and her big mouth! Why'd she have to volunteer me?" He put on a squeaky Claire-voice. "Mr Snipe, sir, can we help the archaeologists sort out their finds?"

He scraped angrily at the piece of broken school dinner china with his washing-up brush.

"Oh, stop moaning, Oswald," said Tom. "They dug up the old toilets this morning – at least you're not sieving dead maggots from ancient dried-up poo."

Oswald turned pale and backed away. Just then Samantha breezed in with a radiant smile.

"Hi boys, how are you getting on?" she asked.

"Fine!" they chorused.

But Samantha was already in the next room where Claire was working on the finds database. First Tom and then Oswald (none too quietly) crept over to the door to find out what Claire and Samantha were talking about.

"The database is going fine!" Claire was saying. "But I was

wondering if they've finished the reconstruction of the adult's skull yet?"

"Reconstruction – what's that?" Oswald whispered to Tom. "Does that mean they're going to put flesh on it?"

"Er, clay, I think," said Tom, frowning. "They make a plaster cast of the skull and then – er, I'm not sure..."

Two weeks later all was revealed.

It was the last day of term and the archaeologists were presenting their finds in the school hall to an audience of parents and children. Professor Digby was explaining the very procedure that had puzzled Tom.

"...and they build up layers of clay to match the muscles. Not forgetting the plaster eyeballs, of course. As you can see from this photo, we used the glass eyeball found on the site, since we're certain that both it and the skull belonged to Margaret Killem."

There was a gasp of horror as Professor Digby clicked a button and an image of a partly fleshed skull with one staring plaster eyeball and one shiny glass eyeball appeared on the screen.

"Cor!" said Oswald.

"Cool!" said Tom. "I bet every time her eye fell out she lost a pupil!"

"Ssh!" said Claire. "I'm trying to make notes!"

"And now here is Kevin Heap to explain what we know about the skull."

The Professor nudged Kevin, who dug nervously in his pocket and fished out a crumpled sheet of paper.

"Er, yes, we were surprised to find the remains of an adult female but the identification was made as a result of research by Samantha."

At this point all eyes turned to Samantha, who switched on her most dazzling smile. Meanwhile Kevin was trying to make sense of his own handwriting.

"Er, um, Samantha found the last will and testament of Margaret Killem:

'I, Margaret Killem, being of sound body and mind' ... oh yeah, here's the crucial bit ... 'do freely confess that in my lifetime I have treated children cruelly. I have beaten them without just cause and do hold the death of three of them from disease upon my conscience. Therefore I endow all my wealth and worldly goods to a charity to purchase books for poor children and my body I direct to be interred in the grounds of my former school.'"

There was a hushed silence. "And this," said Norman Castle, proudly pointing to a muffled object on the table, "is what we reckon Margaret Killem looked like as based on her skull. I s'pose this will be the first time you lot 'ave clapped eyes on the woman."

He deftly removed the cloth to reveal a clay face staring stonily at the audience.

There was a murmur that ran round the audience, getting louder and louder until it turned into a buzz and then an explosion of excited conversation.

"It's Mr Snipe!" gasped Oswald.

"Yeah," said Tom, "those are his squinty little eyes and beaky nose and I'd know them jug ears anywhere!"

"*Silence!*" thundered Mr Snipe, looking very uneasy. "I confess the face does bear a certain resemblance, but I suppose this could be explained by the fact that there is a connection. Er, I wasn't going to say this but ... Margaret Killem was my great-great-great-grandmother."

There was a renewed flurry of voices.

"*Shut up, shut up, shut up!*" roared Mr Snipe, turning crimson and hopping up and down.

"Well, I'll be jiggered!" said Norman.

Everyone crowded out of the hall, still chatting excitedly. Mr Snipe remained behind – he was shaking and dabbing his forehead with a spotted purple hankie. Nearby, Miss Meek, who was also the school librarian, was quizzing the Professor on whether the charity was still in existence and whether there might be funds for the school library.

"They say," said Oswald thoughtfully, "that cruelty runs in families."

"Oh, that's rubbish!" said Claire. "But I bet Mr Snipe knew about the old school all the time. And it's funny that they were both teachers – and in the same place."

"Hey," said Tom, "maybe they ought to put Mr Snipe in a museum too!"

And they all laughed.

Magnificent museums

Museums are no longer stuffy tomb-like vaults full of objects in dusty glass cases and stuffy scholars who ought to be exhibits.

They're interactive, cool, happening places where you can really *experience* the past. In the Jorvik Centre in York, for example, you can see a reconstruction of a Viking site complete with talking people, and sniff realistic chicken droppings and watch a Viking using an outside toilet (by the way, the Vikings used moss as toilet paper).

COME BACK WITH MY MOSS!

And there's a museum at the pleasantly named "Headsmashedin", in Alberta, Canada, where you can experience a reconstruction of bison stampeding over a cliff during a Native American hunt. The interesting name comes from a legend that a warrior tried to catch a falling bison. It was a brave attempt but the warrior must have been one lemon short of a pancake … and that's how he must have looked afterwards. In the future, museums will probably use virtual reality technology to give you the sensation of strolling through an ancient building excavated by archaeologists.

But what exactly *is* the future of archaeology? Well, in the near future you can find out … by reading the next page!

EPILOGUE:
NO FUTURE IN THE PAST?

Archaeology has taught us many things about the way people lived and what they believed – but there's one awesome lesson that we've learnt about ourselves and *it's not very nice*...

HUMANS DESTROY THINGS! We're champion wreckers! As you know, people loot tombs and plunder ancient ruins. But most tragic of all is when people try to protect the past and *still* manage to destroy it.

Remember the story of Smenkare's mummy? Archaeologists wanted to preserve and treasure the battered body, but they broke it and poor Smenkare was smashed for all eternity.

And archaeology itself is a form of destruction. If you dig up a site then you're going to break through the ancient layers, so that future archaeologists will find them harder to study. That's why modern archaeologists often leave part of a site for future generations to explore.

The awesomely awful news

Thousands of ancient sites are in danger. Modern

buildings have deep foundations that break through the archaeological layers. Archaeologists often find themselves digging against time, trying to make a record of a site before builders move in and bury everything in concrete.

Dams create lakes that cover old sites.

Farmers plough up old sites...

The good news
Most countries have laws that protect archaeological sites from robbery or development. And millions of people are really keen on archaeology. They watch archaeology on TV and visit digs and tour museums.

More awful news
Even when an archaeological site has been expertly excavated, it can still be in danger! And the danger comes from the very people who are so interested

in it. Thousands of trampling tourists are wearing sites out – after all, ancient tombs were meant to be quiet as the grave. In the 1980s, the tomb of Nefertari in Egypt had to be restored at enormous cost because the breath of visitors contains spit and the moisture had damaged the paintings. I expect too many visitors were a-coffin in the tomb.

The future of archaeology

Having read this book, you may feel that archaeology sounds awesomely gruesome. Well, yes – but hopefully you'll agree that it's awesomely fascinating too. Basically, archaeology is on the side of the good guys and no doubt future archaeologists will use the latest computer and geophysics technology to save the world's ancient sites for future generations. And that means, with luck, there'll be a great future for the past!

Further information

Young Archaeologists' Club

You can be a member if you're under 16. You'll get involved in local clubs, read a magazine and go on archaeological activity holidays.

Contact:
The Young Archaeologists' Club
St Mary's House
66 Bootham
YORK
YO30 7BZ
e-mail: yac@britarch.ac.uk
web site: www.britarch.ac.uk/yac

Some cool archaeology web sites

There are loads of archaeology websites plus more for museums and many of the places mentioned in this book have a web site. Here are some of our favourites:

www.digonsite.com – the site for DIG Magazine has plenty of archaeological info

www.ancientegypt.co.uk – this great site is dedicated to Ancient Egypt (so how come you've guessed that already?)

www.kidsdigreed.com – this cool interactive site is based on a US Civil War dig but there's plenty about archaeologists and how they study a site

www.pastexplorers.org.uk – there's loads here about how archaeologists work

www.show.me.uk – is THE place to go for UK museums info and there are articles on archaeology too.